100 Hacks for Business Growth

JAMES VINEETH

www.jamesvineeth.com

ISBN 13 : 978-93-5346-174-4

James Vineeth

December 2018

100 Hacks for Business Growth

DEDICATION

I dedicate this Book to my Beloved Family. My wife Sheeba James who has always got my back. Thanks to the patient listening when I share my insights to see if that inspires people or not ☺. She has played a crucial role in bringing the best out of me; My Son Noah James who motivates me by believing that I am a "Super Dad".

My Dad Mr. Michael who taught me the importance of walking your talk; My Mom Sweety who taught me that there is no short-cut to success; My Sister Vinolia who taught me to beat all the odds in life and aim high; My Niece Sheryl, who inspires me by balancing academics and sports.

My Mother in law Mrs. Victoria Prabudass who Prays for my Growth every day. My Siblings in law Richard and Sherin who have been a source of inspiration and support all the time.

CONTENTS

Emotional Intelligence

Business Leadership

Redefining Self

ACKNOWLEDGMENTS

All Praise and Glory and Honour belongs to the Lord Almighty for enabling me and equipping me to be what I am today.

My heartfelt thanks and Gratitude to all my Clients who trusted in my Business Coaching and Training Services. Working with each and every one of them has given me exposure in bringing my insights together as one power packed book.

I take this opportunity to express my Gratitude to the Dynamic Business Forum located in Coimbatore, India for their Trust, Love, and Wishes.

I am ever thankful to my Extended Family who has motivated me and appreciated me for my work. Uncles, Aunts, Sisters, Brothers and all of them.

How can I miss thanking my Teachers and Mentors? From my Schooling till Graduation, I was Blessed enough to have the best Teachers who not only taught me Education but also Life Skills that shaped me.

It is very apt to thank my Spiritual Mentors and Pastors who have guided me in the right path and shared Words of Wisdom that enlightened me.

Last but not least, I thank all my friends who believed that there is a Coach and an Author lying within me. Special mention - "Friends for Life Group" - people who showed me the real meaning of Friendship.

MINDSET

1 BELIEVE IN NEXT LEVEL

The very first principle to Grow is to believe in the NEXT LEVEL. Businesses fail to progress when the top leaders fail to consider that there is room for improvement.

What really makes them reach this un-resourceful state is a feeling of being overwhelmed.

Their Conversations are like . . .

- ✓ I am doing too many things.
- ✓ I have to do things myself.
- ✓ You don't know what I am going through.
- ✓ It's easy to give ideas and feedbacks.
  But challenges are many to execute them.
- ✓ I have enough experience to tell you – that it can't be better than this.

To bring a massive transformation in an Organization, believing in the Next Level of growth is mandatory. Those who fail to acknowledge the space available for improvement will not only stop working for the Next Level but also make their colleagues to be blinded to those possibilities.

** List down three areas of Next Level Growth for your Business / Division / Branch

Illustration:

Sam is the Head of Sales.

The Company has three verticals, and one of them is not performing well. He thinks his team is doing everything they can to get the best result and yet this particular vertical is not showing Growth.

During the Mid-Year Review, CEO and other leaders are confronting Sam about the declined growth of this particular division.

Sam does not see that there is a Next Level and room for improvement.

There is a difference between:

"*Doing* our best and
Assuming that we are doing our best"

and

"Being *Proactive* about Growing and
Being *Reactive* about past Results"

Being *open-minded* and being *Coachable* is undoubtedly the key to believe in the Next Level of Growth.

2 DON'T FULFILL RESPONSIBILITY

Teach your team not to fulfill the responsibility. Sounds Strange, isn't it?

Yes. Organizations don't grow when people fulfill only their responsibility – Stagnated and not growing. (Survival Mode)

The point is fulfilling responsibility is just not enough. We need to Coach our Leaders to "Take Responsibility" and go the Extra Mile.

We need to Orient, our team about the differences between

Fulfilling Responsibility
vs
Taking Responsibility

Great leaders are created when they stand-up, step-up, take greater responsibilities and shoulder each other for the collective growth of the Organization.

Now that's called a Growth Culture!

** Time to train your team!

Illustration:

There are four designations in ABC Company.

- Executive
- Supervisor
- Manager
- Director

Roy joins the team as a Supervisor.

If he thinks working as a Supervisor is just enough for his Growth, then he will be stuck to the role of the Supervisor forever.

He needs to think, act and work like a Manager (Taking Responsibility). This will give him the best learning experience and eventually he will be reaching his next level preparing himself for that role already in advance.

And the journey continues. He will be working for the Next Level all over again.

Expectation: *Promotion First & Action Next*
Reality: *Action First & Promotion Next*

** Train your team to take actions before their Promotion.

3 SELF-LEADERSHIP MASTERY

Entrepreneurs and CXOs are leading other leaders to produce results. However, it is essential for them to hit the mastery level when it comes to how they Lead themselves.

Leadership is all about inspiring and influencing. It is vital to inspire oneself before getting better in inspiring others.

Here are the 4 Self Leadership questions every leader should answer to hit the mastery level in Self-Leadership.

1. Will I follow Myself?
   (A Straight Yes / No)

2. Who is My Role Model?
   (List the Names / If no existing role models, skip to the next question)

3. What are the Qualities of my Role Model?
   (List the Qualities / If no existing role models, list down the expected qualities)

4. Do I have those Qualities? If not what should I do to develop them?
   (This answer is Your PGP – Personal Growth Plan)

4 TREAT PEOPLE DIFFERENTLY

We deal with People. We do not work in an office that is equipped only with Robots. Our productivity and efficiency are much dependent on human interactions.

Business Owners and Top Leaders fail at leading people when they take the "One Size Fits all" approach.

The two most common errors in motivating people are

- Using the *Same Strategy to Motivate Everyone*
- Assuming what *Motivates me will Motivate Others*

Well, Different People have Different Drives.

- *Some are Motivated when you Confront them and Guide them*
- *Some are Motivated when you give a Pep Talk*
- *Some are Motivated when you provide Personal Attention*
- *Some are Motivated when their work has a Noble Cause*
- *Some are Motivated when they are Incentivized Greatly*
- *Some are Motivated when a Promotion is Assured*

** Identify what drives each and every one in your team and treat them differently according to their Drives.

Illustration:

Joseph likes it when his immediate Boss points at his mistakes and corrects him then and there.

Ben does not like to be corrected through his teammates. He prefers a 1 to 1 conversation to talk about his shortcomings.

Jones likes it when the CEO gives him a special task to be finished within the next 6 months to be qualified for a hike or promotion.

Varun is super excited about the new incentive scheme that the Company has launched. He is least bothered about the promotions.

Tharun so badly wants to get that Rolling Trophy next month. For him, incentives and promotions are secondary. Recognition and Appreciation is his main drive to victory and extraordinary performance.

5 R.P.R.M.

R.P.R.M. stands for *Receive Pressure, Release Motivation.* Sadly, in today's corporate scenario we see leaders who Receive Pressure and Release Pressure ☹

The more they receive pressure from the market / environment and surroundings, the more they release pressure to their teammates. This disturbs the work environment and directly impacts productivity.

So how do we let go of our Stress?

Well, develop ways to bust your pressure. Yelling at your team will only make the situation worse. And it will not inspire the team to work harder proactively.

It is no justice to treat our subordinates as Scape-Goats for the issues we have faced as leaders in the Business Environment.

** Most importantly Coach your other Team Leaders to withhold pressure and release positivity to their subordinates. The team that enjoys working with the leader will eventually enjoy working with each other.

6 KNOW WHY PEOPLE WORK LIKE CRAZY FOR THEIR COMPANY

Some Employees work like crazy for their company. They are super loyal, ever resourceful and happy to carry forward new responsibilities without hesitation with a positive attitude.

Have you ever wondered what makes them be very resourceful and happy at Work?

Well, there are three types of Employees:

1. The ones that long for love and affection. (Involves when their team members care for them)

2. The ones that long for respect and honour. (Involves when they are part of a winning team)

3. The ones that apply their talents and make a difference at Work. (Involves when they know their abilities and the organization values their efforts)

** Love your Team Members
** Respect your Team Members
** Give importance to their Opinions
** Let them apply their talents at Workplace
** They will work like Crazy for you (Work with Passion and Full involvement)

7 INFLUENCING THE MILLENNIAL GENERATION

It is clear – The Company that is good at Leading the Millennials will accelerate Fast-Track Growth.

What we need to know about Leading them?

- ✓ Get active on Social Media – Millennials like to share happenings of the organization in Social Media.
- ✓ If you reward them – They may share it on their Social Wall – *Positive Branding.*
- ✓ If you don't treat them well – They may share it on their Social Wall – *Negative Branding.*
- ✓ You really need to earn their Trust.
- ✓ Use Tech tools like C.R.M., E.R.P, E-Mails, Web Conferences, E-Learning Solutions and more.
- ✓ Don't talk about them… Instead, talk to them.
- ✓ Have open & honest conversations with them
- ✓ Give them specific inputs for development.

- ✓ Avoid stereotyping them.
- ✓ Give them individual attention.
- ✓ Give them the freedom to showcase their Creativity.
- ✓ Listen to them – Genuinely.

** Make your Organization Millennial Friendly.
They are the ones who will be bridging Gen X and Gen Z.

8 CELEBRATE BREAKDOWNS

Breakdowns are when things are not going the way they are expected. A positive Entrepreneur looks at failure as a Breakdown.

And when there are Breakdowns, the team has to celebrate it – Approach with passion, positivity and high energy. Sounds strange again? Well, that is what it takes to convert Breakdowns into Breakthroughs.

The very reason to celebrate the Breakdown is to find what caused us the Breakdown, so we don't fail again because of the same reason and can bounce back with the corrected course of action.

Get Serious with Breakdowns	Celebrate your Breakdowns
• People are pressurized • People blame each other • Not inquiring into what's missing • No learning from mistakes • No corrected course of actions • Same mistakes could be repeated again.	• People are energized • People take responsibility • Inquiring into what's missing • Definite learning from mistakes • Definite corrected course of actions • No more repeated mistakes. Make fresh mistakes.

** Time for Celebration.
Love your Breakdowns. Success will love you Back.

Illustration:

Rohan and team hit a Breakdown due to Poor Sales.

As they celebrate the Breakdown as a team, they inquire into the lessons from the Breakdown.

They ask Positive Proactive Questions such as:

- ✓ What is Missing?
- ✓ If we have to relive this month all over again, what would we do differently?
- ✓ What are the three major lessons we learned from this Breakdown?
- ✓ How can the Next Month be different from the previous one?

And they came up with Positive answers such as:

- ✓ Believing that we will win was Missing.
- ✓ We thought every inquiry we get will convert. Our current conversion ratio is 3:10. Therefore in order have 50 Orders, our team needs to generate 170 Inquiries during the first 20 Days of the Month.
- ✓ When we know, we are not on track, we will ask for support!

9 EMOTIONS & ASSOCIATIONS

Emotions are what make us Human Beings. For every work we do, and for every area of our Lives, we attach Emotions. Those emotions determine whether we are having a fruitful, positive uptime or disempowering downtime.

The flipside of a winning leader and a winning department is a positive emotion; Flipside of a losing leader and a losing department is a negative emotion.

List down three things that are *working- well* in your Business now:

1.

2.

3.

List down three things that are *not working* in your Business now:

1.

2.

3.

Find out what Emotions you have Associated / Linked / Attached to the *What's Working column* – I bet they are all Positive Emotions.

When you think of those Divisions / Departments / Tasks, you get a positive feel or even an adrenaline rush.

Now, find out what Emotion you have Associated / Linked / Attached to the *What's Not Working* column – I bet they are all Negative Emotions.

When you think of those Divisions / Departments / Tasks, you get a negative feeling and eventually reach a Un-Resourceful State.

As a Business Leader, it is essential and vital for you to identify those negative emotions - Commit to breaking the pattern – Make a list of positive emotions – Now begin to associate those positive emotions with the not working areas. Every time you catch yourself with such negative emotions, you need to practice switching back to positive emotions.

If you develop a positive emotion in the not working areas, it will empower you to turn things around.

Fun Illustration:

Think of your Favorite Food:

- Ice Cream
- Chicken Burger
- Tandoori Chicken
- Grilled Vegetables
- Anything of your choice

You can realize that you have associated a Positive Emotion to your favorite food and it instantly changes your body language and expressions.

You need to condition yourself to associate such Positive Emotions with your *not working areas* and get excited in giving your 100% to turn things around.

GETTING THE SYSTEMS IN PLACE

10 STOP FIREFIGHTING

Entrepreneurs and CXOs are called to multiply results by getting their team to do more in less time.
(Increase Effectiveness and Efficiency of their team).

Firefighting is a perilous trap to Scaling-Up. It makes Business Leaders exhausted in the process of getting things done by themselves due to lack of a well-built team, and not letting the business run on systems.

Since everything depends on them, they get overwhelmed, develop Stress, and it limits the business from growing massively.

Firefighting Model

- ✓ You Drive Everything
- ✓ Decision Making is Slow
- ✓ Breakdown brings down the Morale
- ✓ Constantly being Nagged
- ✓ YOU are IN the Process – Overwhelmed
- ✓ People are Self-Centered
- ✓ Numbers are used to Defining Victory and Failure
- ✓ Lack of Direction

11 BELIEVE IN AUTO-PILOT MODE

Your business may not run without you. But your business can run without your intervention for silly & repeated things that drain your Energy.

Conditioned Systems & Programmed Success:

You can condition each and every system in your business by programming the decisions to be taken for different situations. This is more like a one-time investment. You just have to set your systems right and put it into practice.

Do not violate them yourself. Intervene only when the odd cases that are not pre-defined arises.

Automated Model

- ✓ System Drives Everything
- ✓ Pre-Automated IFs, BUTs, YESs & Nos
- ✓ Learning from Mistakes is Cultured!
- ✓ Only Monitoring is Needed
- ✓ YOU are ON the Process – Effortless
- ✓ People are Mission Centered (Purpose)
- ✓ Numbers are used for Analysis & Action
- ✓ VISION Drives the Organization!

12 EXCEL IN WHAT YOU DO

Teach your team:

- If you do sloppy work, no one would want you.
- If you excel in what you do, everyone would want to work with you.

An organization should be a place where every individual is coming together for the collective growth of the team. In the due process, they find their talents, support each other and make way for human development.

As iron sharpens iron, team members make a difference in each other's lives by Inspiring them towards Personal Excellence.

Some Interesting Pointers:

- ✓ Excellence is being at their Best.
- ✓ The only trap of Leadership Development is comparison.
- ✓ Everyone in your team may not be the Best. But they can be at their Personal Best.
- ✓ The Objective of every team is to Deliver High-Performance Results.
- ✓ At the same time, they need to work with an Objective of everyone working towards Overall Excellence.
- ✓ Both these Objectives may seem different, but they go hand in hand and will support the overall Growth of the Organization.

13 RESPONSIBLE COMMUNICATION

Leadership and influence don't have anything to do with age, gender, caste, creed, looks, etc.

It is all about Inspiring People. Since this is all about Inspiring, Communication plays a crucial role in passing on that Burning Passion and energy to your team members.

For any great team, one of the most essential attributes should be that of Responsible Communication.

Now, what is that?

It is to have a Blame-free Communication.
Do not be a person who blames others.

It all starts with this simple principle:

- ✓ *I too am responsible for everything that happens around me.*
- ✓ *Though the situation could be external, there could be things I could have done differently to avoid such events/happenings.*

** Practice Responsible Communication at Workplace
** Ban Blameful Words at Workplace
** Introduce few New Words at Workplace
** See how things Change at Workplace

Fun Illustration:

Blameful Communication	Responsible Communication
• Somebody Stole my Phone.	• I lost my Phone.
• Moses said he will send the Mail by 5 P.M.	• I did not follow up Moses closely to ensure the Work.
• The market is very dull.	• We should work Harder.
• That's not My Problem.	• I could have done something about it.
• The canteen food sucks.	• Let me give a written feedback to the in-charge about the quality of food.

14 POSITIVE COMMUNICATION

Just like Responsible Communication, Positive Communication is yet another essential attribute to every Entrepreneur & CXO. We need to ensure everyone in the Organization is Coached on Positive Communication.

As Emotions influence how we feel, the words we choose influences the emotions we go through. Therefore, it is vital to maintain the culture, environment, and positivity of the organization by choosing the right words in describing a problem, process or a situation.

It all starts with these simple principles:

- ✓ *We become what we Speak.*
- ✓ *The words we choose, determine how we feel.*

** Practice Positive Communication
** Ban Negative Words
** Introduce New Positive Words
** See how things Change (Cultured Positivity)

Fun Illustration:

Negative Communication	Positive Communication
• Oh, God. It's Monday, and we need to send that Proposal.	• It was a great Weekend, and I am excited I have a Job that I love.
• That Customer? Ooohh. *Irritating Customer.* I feel like running away.	• That Customer? Wow. *Challenging Customer.* I am all geared up Now.
• This is repeated Work. So boring.	• Repetition is the Key to Excellence. I am going to be better at this.

15 DON'T BUY BULL SH*T

Ha Ha! I know this sounds crazy and funny. I am referring this term to reasons and justifications.

1. Don't give yourselves reasons as to why your Business cannot achieve XX Results

2. Don't buy Reasons from your team as to why they were not able to achieve XX Results

And let me differentiate *Reasons* vs. *Lessons Learned* here.

Reasons basically are those blameful communications and negative communications that describe why you failed and makes you feel as if this is entirely unavoidable and it is okay to fail. It will make you feel comfortable being mediocre.

Lessons Learned are those that come from celebrating your Breakdowns. They are actions that you ought to do differently to achieve results in the immediate future. Those responsible communications and positive communications empowers you to bounce back.

** Self-Deception is when you are Convinced that there is nothing you can do to change the End Results.

16 BECOME A COACH

Entrepreneurs and CXOs have several hats to Change – Chief Executive Officer, Boss, Team Leaders, Friend, Mentor, Well-Wisher, Colleague, Head and much more.

Out of all this, one of the most crucial role to be played is the role of a Coach.

Yes, you lead your team to success not only by giving a Vision to them but also Coaching and aligning them towards that Vision during each and every interaction.

** What Coaching Does?

- ✓ Brings a 3rd Person's Point of View
- ✓ Adds New Perspective and Dimension
- ✓ Asks Empowering Questions that give Proactive answers.
- ✓ Helps Employees to realize where they are lagging by answering simple questions.

** Ask Powerful Questions Like.

- ✓ What is Missing?
- ✓ What needs to be done, for us to reach that XX Results.
- ✓ How badly do we want to fail or lose to take a Corrective Action in this Area?
- ✓ If we have to re-do this again, what will we do differently?

EMOTIONAL INTELLIGENCE

17 BECOMING PEOPLE FRIENDLY

Every business owner needs to know when to empower their team aggressively for results and when to embrace them with love and affection.

You need to become a People Friendly Person – Someone who people will love to hang out with. This not only applies within your organization but also externally with Family, Friends and Business Associates – Clients, Vendors, Forums, etc.

If people love to talk to you, spend time with you, they would like to do business with you as well.

How to be People Friendly?

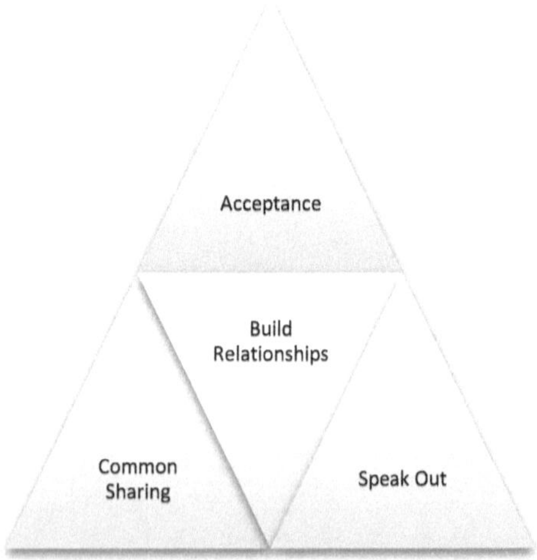

A. Accept People

- ✓ Don't accept People for that they Do
- ✓ Accept People for Who they Are
- ✓ Learn to accept people Unconditionally
- ✓ Come out of the Conditions apply Relationships (Breaking Expectations)
- ✓ If you want others to accept you the way you are; You need to accept them the way they are.

B. Common Sharing

- ✓ We all like to Speak what we love the Most.
- ✓ We need to develop familiarity with topics that excites others to have interesting conversations with them.
- ✓ If you don't want to bore others, you need to find topics of common interest to spend the time well.
- ✓ We tend to like those who share Similarities with us, and it all starts with Conversations.

C. Speak-Out

- ✓ Have Open and Honest Communication with People
- ✓ If you have a problem with someone, deal it with them directly. Do not bad-mouth.
- ✓ When you share such things do it Politely and Gently (Practice Responsible and Positive Communication)
- ✓ Be Real and do not carry or hide behind a Mask that says everything is alright, but deep inside you are fuming with hurt and hatred.

18 CONNECT WITH PEOPLE

Be it leading a team or selling a product/service, the first step is to connect with people.

Great leaders connect with people with ease. And how do you do that?

Well here is my Tip (I call it the *Leaky Bucket Tip)*

Here you go. Every person we come across is like a leaky bucket. There is this one leaky point you need to unplug, and then the water keeps gushing out.

Same way there are these leaky points for every person (Topics, areas of interest, things they are passionate about, things that excites them and the like)

You just need to build compatibility with them by asking the right questions and then you got them speaking for a long time. All you need to do now is to genuinely listen to them and that's the best way to connect with anyone instantly and build Rapport.

** Ask Questions like . . .

- ✓ What made you Start this Business?
- ✓ Where are you from?
- ✓ What's unique about that place?
- ✓ What is your No.1 Product / Service?
- ✓ I saw your Ad on TV last week. It was Brilliant! How did you get that Concept?
- ✓ Your website is stunning. Who designed it?
- ✓ What's new for the New Year?

DIY:

Make a list of 5 Business Categories

(You are meeting these people from 5 different Business Backgrounds).

Now make a list of Conversation Starters.

How can you use the Leaky Bucket tip and shoot interesting questions to each person from each Business Category and get them to talk for more time?

Business Category	Conversation Starter

19 BE LIKE P.M.

Every Entrepreneur and CXO should be like P.M.
P.M. in Growth Hacking Scenario is referred to *Possibility Making Machine.*

Your primary job as a leader is to give the hope and belief to your team that *"It Is Possible."*

It is common and natural for team members to lose hope and to believe that it is difficult to achieve. Our job as business leaders is to create Unlimited Possibilities for them.

Every time we communicate with the team, they need to walk out with a Conviction of *"WOW this is really going to happen, and we will find a way to Win."*

When people come to us with problems in their hands, they need to walk out with solutions and possibilities. This doesn't mean we need to give them ideas to implement, but it is all about creating a positive space in your organization. In this culture, people don't just talk about problems but are able to come up with possible solutions and ideas by themselves with a hope that Breakthrough is a few steps away.

It is that Powerful Positive Space we need to create by being a source of inspiration – *Possibility Making Machine.*

20 DELIVER AWESOME PEP TALKS

CEOs are known for PEP Talks. Your words should move people. It needs to spread that burning sense of passion to others.

Now how do you make that talk awesome and peppy?

This is not about using strong words, playing a background music, speaking in high volume or anything of that sort. This is all about emotion & impact.

Ordinary People when asked to give a Talk:
They ask themselves *what I can talk?*

Vs.

Great People when asked to give a Talk:
They ask themselves *what do I want them to Get?*

Work Backwards:

Step 1 – List the Key Outcomes of your Talk (KO)

How to figure this out?

1. List down three things you want them to get.

2. After your talk, if someone asks any of your audience, "What was the talk about ?" what do you want them to answer?

Step 2 – Build a Story Line for Each Key Outcome. What example or illustration you want to use for each KO?

Step 3 – Choose your Emotion. For each story / illustration you can choose the Emotions you want to use.

Fun Illustration:

Step 1 (KO)
Outcome 1 – Never Give Up

Step 2 Story Line
Talk about top 3 Rejections faced by XX Celebrity.

Step 3 Emotion
Use the Emotion of Passion

Note: The above example has only one **KO**. Every talk can have a minimum of 3 KOs and a maximum of 5 KOs.

DIY:

Prepare a Sample PEP talk with 5 Key Outcomes:

Key Outcomes (KO)	Story Line	Emotion

21 FOCUS ON CHARACTER & PERFORMANCE

For a leadership culture to be followed in your organization, ensure you give importance to both Character and Performance.

If you look deep enough, you will be able to find that some employees are very good at accomplishing results but they bring down the morale with poor character – Not cooperating with people, not adhering to the policies, not following guidelines and violating the rules of the game. Somehow, they manage to get away by producing results, and due to that no one really bothers to confront them.

In the same way, you will also find people who are very good in character – Adhering to the policies, being kind and loyal. But they fail to produce results. A great human being who is not contributing to the growth is still a burden for the company.

So give importance to review both Character and Performance. If your core team is built with people who are good at both Character and Performance, your organization is *Blessed and Poised to Grow.*

** Make a list of People who are good with Character & Performance.

22 USE CAPTURE TOOL

I always mention "Human beings are Forgetting Machines." When your brain is super creative and is pumping out Breakthrough ideas, you need to Capture them!

I bet you have experienced this – You had a brilliant idea when you were driving/talking to a client / taking a shower and later you were sitting at your office trying to recollect that creative idea and . . . . . you are just not able to remember it.

Great leaders use capture tool. It is a simple and effective habit of noting down your ideas as they pop up.

How amateurs do it – They note down ideas in different areas. Note Pad, Laptop, Mobile, Calendar, etc. They are all over the place. Ideas are written but will they be processed?

How Pros do it – They mostly use only one place to note down their Ideas. Preferably an app or tool that syncs across different devices. They can note down the ideas using their mobile and later pick it up from their Laptop and resume working on it!

They also use Tags / Folders / Labels to categorize their ideas for better use. Each idea is treated like a Billion Dollar Breakthrough and does not expire without implementation or giving it a shot.

** Start Capturing Today!
Begin with using a couple of tools today and after a week, compare them and decide to use whichever better suits your needs.

23 EDIFY YOUR TEAM

Morally, improve the quality of your team members. Some business owners yell at their Core team in front of their subordinates. This brings down the morale, and it takes time for people who are emotionally disturbed by this, to get back to normal state of mind and work optimally.

It is wise to confront your team in private - *A separate meeting with them.* And if you notice that they have done their best and have set new standards, it is time you edify them – *Appreciate them Openly in front of their subordinates for the outstanding Contribution. Nothing can beat this level of Motivation.*

Sadly, we see the opposite happening in Companies these days. The Core team get yelled in public and appreciated in Private.

We just have to swap these two to keep the team high in Spirit.

** When was the last time you appreciated your Core Team Openly?

Will you do it today?

BUSINESS LEADERSHIP

24 CREATE AND LIVE THE VISION

Vision is what inspires people to grow along with your organization in the long run. When it comes to Vision, there are three types of Businesses.

- ✓ There is no clear Vision – Keeps Changing.
- ✓ There is a Vision, but no one talks about it.
- ✓ There is a Vision & it drives People.

Vision needs to be Lived – Yes, from the CEO till the last person in the hierarchy, everyone must believe that we are marching closer towards our Vision and are giving our best to make this possible.

Great business is lead, influenced and inspired by its Vision.

The 4 Way Test for Quality of the Vision:

- ✓ Does it Inspire you? – Management
- ✓ Does it Inspire your Customers?
- ✓ Does it Inspire your Employees?
- ✓ Does it Inspire your Investors?

** Are people believing and living the Vision of your Organization?
Does it Inspire them?

25 VISION CASTING

Vision casting is a continuous process of getting people to believe, visualize and operate to make the Vision come true.

Vision needs to be reinforced in all possible and practical ways through – Display Signage at Office, Vision Discussion during Quarterly Team Meeting, Vision-related Growth Questions during Annual Performance Review and more.

This may look like a simple ritual. But it goes deep in their heart, creates a conviction and makes them belong to the Company, and they gradually begin to treat this Vision like their Vision by making it personal. It gives them an emotional satisfaction of doing something significant with their Lives.

** When was the last time you had a Vision Casting Meeting at your office?

DIY:

Share the Vision of your organization and instruct your team:

Imagine you are there in the Future and we have accomplished our Vision. Being there in that state of fulfillment, share your thoughts on how would you feel achieving such a great thing as a team, organization and an individual.

Illustration:

The Vision for my Team (James Vineeth)

Vision 2035 – *www.jamesvineeth.com*

- ✓ Empower 1 Lakh CXOs to Scale-Up and Run their Business in Auto Pilot Mode
- ✓ Transform 1 Million Leaders through Masterclass and Special Programs
- ✓ Impact 10 Million Lives through Digital Medium

The Vision for our Non-Profit (CSR)

111 (Triple One). Vision 2030 - *www.savetheglobe.info*

- ✓ Impact One Lakh (1,00,000) People's Lives through various Portfolios
- ✓ Sponsor Education for One Thousand Children (1000) through Spread A Smile Project
- ✓ Establish One (1) Educational Institution

During all major Core Team meetings, we Emotionally connect and share how it would be when this becomes a Reality.

26 PLAY THE NUMBERS GAME

As Business Leaders, we must speak the Language of Numbers. The very first thing we need to do is to get rid of adjectives that make things vague.

Words such as

- ✓ Great Work
- ✓ Nice Results
- ✓ Very Bad Market
- ✓ Tried my Level Best
- ✓ Awesome Results
- ✓ More Business
- ✓ Superb Efforts

And the like will get you blinded to look at the Real Numbers.

Core Secret:

What is Fact? Fact is anything and everything that exists in Numbers.

The market is Bad – Is it a Fact?
Well, we need to look into *Numbers.*

- ✓ Last FY – How many inquiries we had?
- ✓ This FY – How many inquires we have?
- ✓ What is the conversion ratio for last year and this year?
- ✓ What is the average deal price for each order last year and this year?

As business owners, we are doing this. But this isn't enough. You need to get your Core Team to do this. Only then you will be running Business based on *Facts* and not *Feelings.*

Illustration:

Frank is a lazy employee. His performance has gone down. (Works in the Production Department)

A wise leader doesn't go by adjectives and emotions. Let's look at the Numbers.

- How many Days Frank has taken off during the last 6 months?
- What was his daily production target vs. achieved target in the Last 6 Months?
- Cross check the No. of productions delays and how many of them come under Frank's portion of work.
- Take out the quality complaints register and cross check for errors in Frank's portion of work.

Bottom Line Finding: Frank is the most productive employee of the Company. However, his Supervisor did not assign enough work for him each day, and he had been treated at par with the new trainees who were on board.

27 WORK WITH PERSONALITY TRAITS

Does Personality have anything to do with Business?
Yes. It does.

There are many personality assessments available today. Each personality has its own positives and shortcomings. Every business owners must take a personality assessment to learn what their traits are.

Traits are characteristics and attributes that naturally come to a person according to their Personality type. Wise people play with their Strengths.

Based on the Personality type, your traits could be

- ✓ Being Creative
- ✓ Being Jovial
- ✓ Working on Complex Ideas
- ✓ Inspiring People
- ✓ Working within thin Deadlines

And much more.

** Take up a personality assessment. Know your Traits.

On a Scale of 1 to 10, rate how well you are using each attribute to the best at your Business.

28 WORK ON PERSONALITY'S SHORTCOMINGS

Every skill / strength will have a Shadow: A dark side to that.

For instance, if a person is highly creative and excited about seeking new challenges and roles, he/she may have problems staying on the go and soon will get bored with the current challenge and long to take on a new challenge to pursue.

There are two ways to overcome the Personality Shortcomings.

1. Create a PGP – Personal Growth Plan that focuses on equipping you to get better at your Shortcomings.

2. Do what you do the best and *delegate/hire* for the rest. Those areas that do not come under your skill set can be mapped to someone else whose personality traits are naturally complementing to the requirements of such roles.

** Get your Core team to take a personality assessment and you can do a self-evaluation whether the right tasks and challenges are assigned to them.

29 DON'T TAKE SWOT FOR GRANTED

Though SWOT assessment is highly popular, businesses fail to learn from their mistakes and miss growing rapidly by taking SWOT for granted.

When was the last time you did a SWOT for your business along with a core team? It has become a habit where we just discuss SWOT verbally during a meeting and think that we have done our part.

During each mid-year review or at least during annual review, it is mandatory that the Core team sits together to work on SWOT for businesses as well as their individual division / product line.

Some Questions to be Answered along with your Core Team:

- ✓ Compared to Competitors what are your Strengths?
- ✓ What is that one thing you are lacking, and it costs your Growth?
- ✓ What are the Opportunities and Threats due to the following factors?
    - o Competition
    - o Political
    - o Economic
    - o Social
    - o Technological
    - o Legal
    - o Environmental

** Time for your Exclusive SWOT meeting with your Core Team.

30 LISTENING TO YOUR CLIENT'S PROBLEMS

You are in Business primarily to Solve a Problem. And by doing this, eventually, you will make money. Never ever forget this simple yet profound truth about the very reason why people like to do business with you.

In today's highly competitive environment, anyone can launch a product in the Market. But growth comes only for those who are addressing the pain points of the end user. And that is precisely why it's an important growth ritual to listen to your client's problems.

Either way, it supports your Growth.

1. If you have a Product / Service that addresses their Problem, you have an inquiry or a sale.

2. If you don't have Product / Service that addresses their Problem, you have identified a market or opportunity for your next Product / Service.

If you are lucky enough, for a short period you can even enjoy a monopoly in the market if no one else has a product or service that addresses the client's pain points like your Product or Service does.

** Meet with your top 25 Clients in the Next 30 Days to listen to their Problems (Future Requirements)

31 GETTING BETTER AT SOLVING PROBLEMS

Well, if you have listened to the problems of your clients and have not done anything about them, things can even start to work negatively for you.

If the client has trusted you enough, they would also develop a hope that you would be doing something about their problems.

You still have creative ways of solving their problems.

1. See what Product / Service you can alter to tailor-fit their needs.

2. Check the feasibility of coming up with a new product / service to address those problems (provided there is enough demand for this or repeatedly other clients are asking for the same solution – market is ready)

3. Simply refer and recommend your vendors or non-competing business associates who are having a ready-made solution to those problems. After all, *what goes around comes around.*

REDEFINING SELF

32 PLANNING LIKE A PRO

We all know this famous quote by "Benjamin Franklin" – *If you fail to Plan, you Plan to Fail.*

Business Owners must be pioneers in planning. They ask the following questions each time they come up with a plan.

- ✓ What needs to be done?
- ✓ Who has to do it?
- ✓ When should it be done?
- ✓ Where should it take place?
- ✓ Why do we need to do it?
- ✓ How to do it?

Everyone in your Core Team should work with this level of clarity, and it all starts from the CEO.

Unless and until things get implemented, a plan is only a *scribbling on the paper*. Therefore, for better implementation, action items and review mechanisms are to be determined in advance.

** When you plan, keep in mind

- ✓ What are the Major Milestones?
- ✓ Who are the Point Persons for each Outcome?
- ✓ What are the Pre-Automated Reviews and Reporting Dates for Each Milestone?
- ✓ What will be the Corrective Actions in case of Lag in Progress?

33 PERFECTION LIMITS PROGRESS

For Human Beings, it is natural to get conscious of our Image. We don't want to lose, and we don't want to be embarrassed. At a psychological level, that limits us.

Surprised? Because we want to do things perfectly, we postpone them to tomorrow and as usual, the tomorrow never comes.

I can give you a whole list of things CXOs postpone just because they are waiting to release a perfect Version.

- ✓ The vision of the company is not framed
- ✓ Their first YouTube video is not released
- ✓ Blogs are still in the making and editing process
- ✓ Business policies are not yet framed
- ✓ Annual magazine has not been released
- ✓ Postponing the company's newsletter release
- ✓ Their first social media Campaign hasn't been launched yet
- ✓ Crafting an Orientation Plan

  And much more . . .

** Every time we think of taking actions for such things, we tell ourselves *"I will not do this now in a hurry. I will take more time and do it really well"* and the perfect time never comes.

Just take actions and release your Version 1.0 and things will start getting better in each Version ☺

34 ORGANIZING & ERGONOMICS

We all know this famous line "A place for everything and everything in its place." One of the best things that can happen to any business is the implementation of 5S Systems. It suits both the manufacturing set up as well as the front office set up.

But it needs to start from the CEO. If you or your team is spending several hours to search documents, files, and other items at the office – That's a sign of not being Organized.

Does this affect Growth?

Indirectly, Yes. You come up with an idea and decide to work on it. As you begin, sooner or later you will be searching and running around for stationery or reference materials or old reports and get upset for wasting time searching for them. This in-turn spoils your state of mind, and eventually, you will lack interest in pursuing the task.

Use Ergonomics at the Workplace.

Productivity and Ergonomics go hand in hand. It is how you can place all the necessary things for a particular task within reach. Doing so saves times, avoids unnecessary movements or running around and lets you stay focused on your task.

** Is your cabin Ergonomically supporting you?
Implement this concept in – Manufacturing, Dispatching, Purchasing, Stocking, Raw Material Storage, etc.

35 EMPATHIZE AT ALL LEVELS

Practice Empathizing with all levels of People involved in your business environment.

- Employees
- Partners / Core Leaders
- Investors
- Customers

Putting yourself in their shoes will help in relating with people better. The better you associate with people, the better you understand their emotions. The more you know their emotions, the better you become in connecting with them.

People don't just work with companies. They choose to work with quality leaders. Knowing people beyond their roles is a rare Quality seen in visionary leaders.

I urge you to be a visionary leader who inspires people and not an ordinary Boss who only thinks of getting people to achieve their targets.

** Empathize with your Team
Learn what matters to them the most.
Know their Aspirations – Dream and Life Goals.
Laugh with them, Celebrate with them.

36 KNOW WHAT STOPS YOU

God has abundantly Blessed each and every one of us with the ability to think and take actions for Growth. But often we don't take actions.

If I ask you to make a list of 10 things you can do today for the betterment of your business, you will get that ready in the next two minutes.

This proves that most of the time we know what needs to be done for the betterment of our lives and businesses. It's just that we don't push ourselves enough to take actions.

Here are some Conversations that stop us:

- ✓ I will get this done some other time / later
- ✓ I will get this done in some other place / different location
- ✓ I don't know if I can really do this myself / Self-Doubt
- ✓ Maybe I'll get a better idea / Discounting the Current Idea

** Once you know what stops you from taking action, You can catch yourself each time when you are limited by these conversations.

37 IDENTIFY YOUR LIMITING PATTERNS

This is a more Personal level of knowing what limits you and in what ways. We can also call it Self-Sabotaging Patterns.

Take time to notice the cycles you go through during each breakdown or a not-working process. We all have our own ways of reacting to things and how we personalize the breakdowns.

Once we are able to find our limiting patterns – The not helpful and un-resourceful way of approaching a breakdown, we can be aware of our limiting patterns and prevent ourselves from going through the same vicious cycles again and again.

** What are your Self Sabotaging Patterns?

How can you break the Pattern to Accelerate Growth?

Illustration:

(Imaginary Characters and Situations)

- ✓ Melvin is Excited to Work on New Challenges.
- ✓ Week One - He is thoroughly Excited about the Role.
- ✓ Great Results – He is Happy and shares with his team about the Positive Experience.
- ✓ Poor Results – Next week the results are very Poor.
- ✓ Breakdown Pattern – During poor performance, Melvin feels that asking for help will make him inferior in front of others and tries to manage things on his Own.
- ✓ Overwhelmed – Due to this, he feels overwhelmed entirely and thinks he is not good enough for the Role.
- ✓ Feeling Stuck – Feeling not good enough and not asking for Support is a dangerous place to be. Now, Melvin needs to work on changing this limiting pattern.

38 CUSTOM FRAME YOUR REPORTING TEMPLATES

CXOs should be on top of the game. I have personally worked with entrepreneurs who have stopped getting regular updates from some of their divisional heads.

When I asked why, here were the answers I got:

- James, I have asked for the report several times, and these people don't give me what I need in the report. Therefore, I have stopped asking for reports and will only look at the end results each month.

- James, the data my team is presenting me are not accurate. Therefore, I stopped asking for reports.

Well, Dear CXO!

This is a one-time thing you need to do. Custom create a reporting template (Weekly – Monthly – Quarterly) for each division. To play the numbers game in business wisely, you need to be on top of the Game. And you need to do this through establishing solid reporting systems.

** Custom Create Reports for

Sales
Purchase
Production
Payments
And More

39 BALANCE LONG RUN AND SHORT RUN

Are you a Long Run Person or Short Run Person? It is about time you find this.

Long Run Person

- ✓ Thinks more about the 5 and 10 Year plans for Business
- ✓ Thinks about Expansion into different Areas
- ✓ Thinks about Future Products and Innovation
- ✓ Think about the Upcoming Trends
- ✓ Not focusing much on Short-Term Stuff

Short Run Person

- ✓ Thinks more about Today's, This Week's and This Month's Tasks
- ✓ Thinks more about Current Growth
- ✓ Think more about the Operational Side of the Business
- ✓ Thinks more about Making enough money for Now
- ✓ Not focusing much on the Long Run Stuff

Well, we are all inclined towards anyone of them. A Wise Business Owner focuses both on the Long Run as well as the Short run – You need to have a plan to Win in Business Today, Tomorrow, Next Month and even after 5 Years.

40 BALANCE PEOPLE AND RESULTS

Are you *People Driven* or the *Results Driven*?
It is about time you find this.

People Driven

- ✓ Gives Importance to People and their Inputs
- ✓ Cares about Job Satisfaction for Everyone
- ✓ Loves People Unconditionally
- ✓ Put People First
- ✓ Put Results Next

Results Driven

- ✓ Gives Importance for Results and Performance
- ✓ Cares about Targets and Winning
- ✓ Loves People if they are Successful
- ✓ Put Results First
- ✓ Put People Next

Well, we are all inclined towards anyone of them. A wise leader creates an excellent balance between both - You need to know when to embrace your team with a hug and when to coach them for results and push them to be at their best.

The (+) s and (–) s of Both the Styles

People Driven

+ Everyone will like you
+ People love to Work

- People will Not Respect You / Take you for Granted
- Missed Deadlines and Goals

Results Driven

+ Team will Win / Achieve Targets
+ People will Respect you as a Leader

- Though they Respect you, they may not like you
- People feel Pressurized at Work

Creating a fine balance between both is something that as CXOs, we need to master!

TECHNOLOGY & BUSINESS

41 TIME FOR MIS / ERP

Are you prepared to Scale-Up?

Earlier in this book, we talked about believing in the next level and preparing for the next level as a business leader. But what about preparing for the next level as an organization?

Investing in Software is Costly!
Not Investing in Software is Costlier!

Why Business Owners Hesitate Investing in a Software?

- ✓ Assume they are Costly
- ✓ Fear of losing Control
- ✓ Skeptical about the difference it brings
- ✓ Not having enough Expertise to Choose the Right One
- ✓ Worried if the Employees will switch from Traditional to Technical Mode

Why Business Owners MUST Invest in a Software?

- ✓ You have Options – Buy a famous Suite related to your Business – Plug & Play, Buy an existing Software and Make few customizations for your Requirement, Custom Create a Software for your Business.

- ✓ You can buy a Complete Suite / ERP or choose to get different Products that suit your requirements only – Sales Module, Accounting Module, HR Module, Etc.

- ✓ Get Real-Time Reports – Stay on top of the Game
- ✓ Helps you to Play the Numbers Game well
- ✓ Automated Reports – Daily, Weekly, Bi-Weekly and all such scheduled reports reach you on time without delay!
- ✓ Get to Details – You will be able to measure and analyze even the smallest piece of information that is affecting your Growth.

** Start listing out software products that are available in the market to see if they can solve your pain points.

42 LEAD NURTURING FLOW – EXPERIENTIAL DESIGN

In every country and every home, they have their own way of welcoming guests. So, what is your company's way of welcoming guests?

Guests – I am referring to the customers and prospects who are visiting your websites, digital storefronts or even making business inquiries through calls and E-Mails.

Do you have *Lead Magnets?*

The first rule in generating inquiries is to set up lead magnets. They are the tools that help you to capture those leads / inquiries.

Some Lead Magnets are:

- ✓ Business Inquiry Form on your Website (Immediate Prospect)
- ✓ News Letter Sign up (Long Term Prospect)
- ✓ Call Logs – Customers calling you for Inquiries (Dedicated Number is advised for better Tracking)
- ✓ Email – A dedicated Mail ID for Inquiries is advised for better Tracking.
- ✓ Posters / Advertisements having Call to Action - Scan QR Code, Call or Mail to avail the offer, Etc.

- ✓ Social Media Advertisements synced with Inquiry Generation Forms.
- ✓ Blogs and Articles written by Experts in your team – Generating Traffic to your Site and Convert in the Long Run.

Design the User Experience!

Right from the moment someone has inquired your product, design a series of experiences that will be created from your brand.

Illustration:

- ✓ Welcome, Note – *Hola! Thank you for the Inquiry.* You have made the right choice. We are excited to share our profile.
- ✓ *Education* + Follow Mail – 1 (Share an Insight and gently follow up on their Requirement)
- ✓ *Education* + Follow Mail – 2 (Share an Insight and gently follow up on their Requirement)
- ✓ Give them an *Exclusive Offer* – If need be.
- ✓ *Thank you for the Order* – In case the order has been closed.

- ✓ *We missed it. Will wait to serve you again.* – Send an acknowledgment even if things don't convert to Business.

- ✓ Add to *Mail List* – Let them get your Newsletters and Insight Mails (Great Companies don't send Emails only to sell products. They send Emails that customers love reading – Insights, Valuable Information, and Offers)

Automate your Process:

Set predefined actions for each step and create an Automated Marketing Process. (Refer to Believe in Auto-Pilot Mode Chapter)

Marketing Automation - Sample:

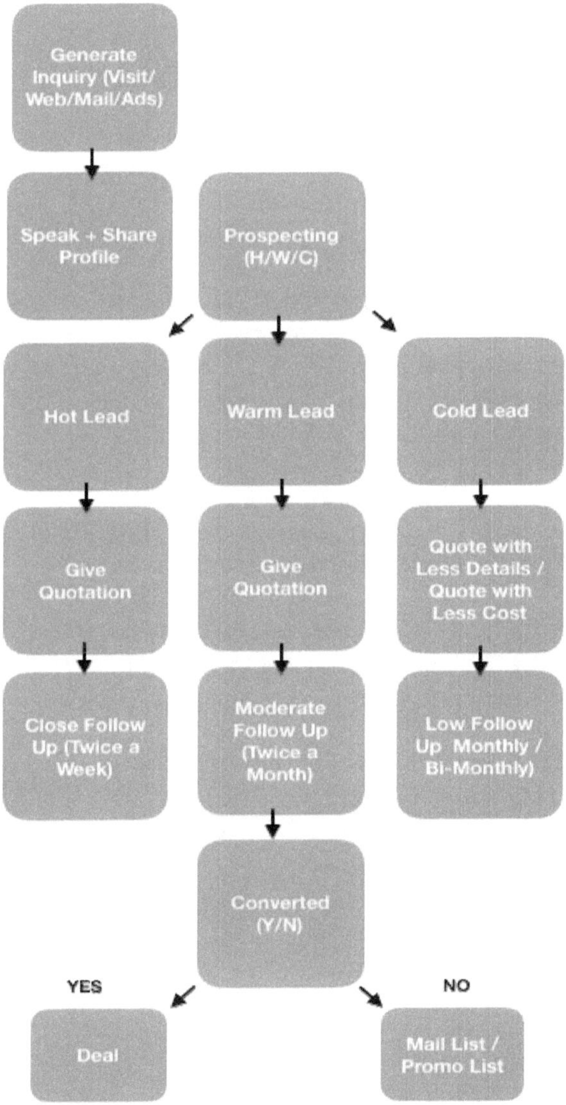

43 BANK ON C.R.M.

Hello, we are living in the 21st Century! It's about time we bring technology to businesses. Enough of following up your sales leads / inquiries with pen, paper or those inquiry ledgers.

Tell you what; This sounds crazy, but I can see many businesses trapped in this area. Most companies I have Coached, when I did a process level consulting on their sales follow up and closure mechanism, I was shocked.

Their Sales Team is not even recording their inquiries on a piece of paper or ledger. Majority of the answers I received when asked about how they follow up are this – *"I will remember each and every inquiry and follow them up every day. I will never forget them. I will be processing this information in my mind".*

Dear CXO! This is a dangerous place to be. I would like to remind you of the two Hacks we discussed in this book earlier.

1. Use the Capture Tool. Whenever you get Ideas, you record them. You will even get thoughts about selling a new product to an existing client – Capture them!

2. Play the Numbers Game. To play this well in Sales, you need to implement C.R.M.

Have you ever calculated the Value of Each Inquiry your Generate?

Let's Say you Participate in an Exhibition to Display your Products and Generate Sales Inquirers.

Participating Expenses in the Exhibition: $1500

No of Inquiries Generated: 500

Cost Spent for One Inquiry: $3

Despite investing money, time and energy, some Companies still miss to professionally manage those 500 Inquiries.

Special Note:

I don't want to sound exaggerating. In fact, to arrive at the actual cost you have to add other expenses such as per day salary for the time spent in the stall, brochure costs and other printing expenses, Travel cum Transporting costs and much more.

ROI on effective implementation of C.R.M. is high.

Take my word for it.

** There are many Customer Relationship Management Suites.

Try one today!

Warning:

- ✓ Just because you buy a C.R.M. suite, it will not solve your Problem of Poor follow up.
- ✓ You need to Ensure your team is feeding the Inquiry Data the same day in the System.
- ✓ You need to sit for Periodical Reviews to look at the Progress Made.
- ✓ Also, ensure Digital Leads (From Website, Social Media Marketing, Etc) are directly getting synced with your C.R.M. suite. Else your team will need to make double entries.
- ✓ Also, set rules and escalation formulae.
  E.g., If there is new Inquiry and the Proposal has not been sent within 24 Hours, you get notified about this. (Or your team generates this report and informs you.)

44 DON'T MISS YOUR SOCIAL MEDIA LEVERAGE

Your customers or end users are on social media. And if you are looking to achieve TOPA – *Top of the Mind Attention* for your brand, get the Social Media leverage.

Funny Fact:

I hope your business has an official page on all social media platforms. If not on all, at least one of them.

If you don't have – Why don't you try visiting any Social Media site now and search for your Brand Name? Your employees or customers or well-wishers would have already created something in your name. So better you create an authentic Official Social Media Page in all the top trending platforms.

You can either run sponsored promotions or keep sharing great content on your wall and get the full leverage without spending a single penny for it.

Most importantly these posts let your customers and end users to engage with your brand in their personal wall (This is such an excellent opportunity to build your brand and achieve TOPA)

** Time to Create / Update / Tweak your Social Media Pages today.

45 LEVERAGE EVERYTHING

Great CXOs know the Power of Leveraging!
If you are working on one initiative, and with the same amount of time, money and energy you can make progress on a few other initiatives, why would you want to miss out?

Well, leveraging everything is more of a mindset. This is not about being scattered in your actions or approach. This is about how to get more done in less time, money & energy.

Some Examples for Leveraging.

- ✓ Record a WOW level Educational Video related to your Business – One-time Investment – Use it repeatedly as Automated Webinars and generate Business Leads forever!

- ✓ Running a Training Session at your Office? Use the same platform to recognize the top Performers of the previous quarter.

- ✓ Going out to Visit a Client? Well, spend more time – Get feedback from them, listen to pain points, get a Social Media Review, Get their consent to shoot a Video Testimonial of them. And also, think on who else you can meet on the way.

** Leveraging everything is a Mind-set. Just keep practicing, and you will get better at it. Soon people will ask you *"How are you able to do so much and where do you find the time for it?"*

PROFITABILITY

46 CREATE YOUR CORE TEAM

In this book, several times I have mentioned "*Core Team.*" Who are they? They are your key leaders.

It can be a mix of your division heads, managers, people who have worked with your company for a longer duration and your top performers. Well, in every organization there is a Core Team. Just that it is not officially announced.

In your mind, you would have considered certain leaders as part of your Core Team but they would not know that you have valued them so much and vice versa. So, make your core team official. Let them know they are important pillars of your organization.

DIY:

- ✓ Create a Core Team
- ✓ Call for the First Meeting
- ✓ Do Vision Casting with them
- ✓ Set up Communication Channels for the Core Team
- ✓ Define Reporting Structures and Routines
- ✓ Any Major Changes you would like to bring, first run it with them.
- ✓ Get them to partner with you to implement new Changes and Policies within the Organization.

47 TREAT EACH DIVISION AS SBU

Treat each Division as SBU – Strategic Business Unit. This will enable people to work as Intrapreneurs – Employees who think, act and work like Entrepreneurs! (High level of Ownership and Involvement).

It is essential to treat each division as a separate revenue center. It's like running multiple business under a holding company (virtual accountability to become debt free and generate profits). Apparently, the first milestone will be to becoming a self-sufficient SBU.

Implementation Hacks:

- ✓ Start with treating one or two Divisions as SBUs as this is going to be new for you.
- ✓ Pick up Performing Divisions, so the performance numbers become Benchmarks for upcoming SBUs
- ✓ Periodically Meet with Intrapreneurs to see how they are Scaling-Up.
- ✓ Equip them with right Training and Coaching to develop an Entrepreneurial Mind-Set.
- ✓ Let them also learn the remaining 99 ways to Hack Growth.

48 FOCUS ON OPERATIONAL MARGINS

Entrepreneurs and CXOs should process profitability numbers in their minds – Playing the Numbers Game.

Every time you talk about growth, expansion, sales, and profits, keep in mind not to get excited about the volume of sales but be wise to look at operationally how much revenue it has generated for your Business.

Product	**Buy Rate**	**Sell Rate**	**OP Margin Amount**	**OP Margin %**
Product A	500	800	300	37.5
Product B	1000	1200	200	16.66
Product C	600	1100	500	45.45

Here, Product C is getting 45% of Operational Margins.

DIY:

- ✓ Make a list of Products / Services you are Offering.
- ✓ Arrive at the Operational Margins for each of them.
- ✓ Let the information sink and let it play in your mind.

Trust me, you will get amazing ideas about

- ✓ What Products / Services to Scale Further?
- ✓ What New Product / Services can you Launch?
- ✓ Is it worth to Borrow Money on Interest and Pump it on a Product that yields less Operational Margin?

And much more . . .

** Time to make this Chart for your Business!

49 MATCH TARGETS WITH MARGINS & EXPENSES

I would like to introduce the BOSP – *Business Operational Success Plan.*

Fixing up Targets – Organizations fix targets based on market analysis, competitor performance, previous year's performance, their team size and sometimes purely on an emotional note.

Arrive at Optimal Budget - Organizations plan for expenses and fix budget based on sales, forecast, competitor performance, previous year's expenses, their team size and sometimes purely on an emotional note.

The BOSP Plan syncs both Sales & Expenses and makes it interdependent.

Step – 1
Arrive at your Actual Expenses for Each Month:
(Reality Check)

Simplified Expenses Tracker (SET)				
Category of Expense	**Needed Expenses**		**Desired Expenses**	
	Amount & Frequency	**Simplified Per Month Exp (SPME)**	**Amount & Frequency**	**Simplified Per Month Exp (SPME)**
1				
2				
3				
4				
5				

Needed Expenses – Your mandatory expenses and unavoidable expenses. You can even bring your long-term expenses into consideration and fit them into the monthly expenses by arriving at the per month cost.

E.g., Salaries, utilities, etc.

Desired Expenses – You wish you can also do these things for your business. They are not Mandatory.

E.g. – Offer Tour, Special Advertisements, Etc.

Bringing everything to Monthly Expenses Mode:

Example : UPS and Battery : Cost 10000
Frequency of Change : 5 Years
Therefore, Per Month Cost is 10000 / 60 Months = 166.66

(When you calculate and convert all your long-term expenses into Monthly Expenses, you get the real picture of how much money your Business needs to Survive and Expand)

Step – 2

Set Business Growth / Sales Targets and also arrive at how much you would be making

(Operational Margin Projection)

Target & Operational Gain							
Product / Service	OP Margin % (A)	Avg Cost (B)	Target Per Year (C)	Target Per Month (D) = (C/2)	Revenue Per Year (E) = (B) * (C)	Revenue Per Month (F) = (B) * (D)	Operational Gain Per Month (G) = (D*A/100)
1							
2							
3							
4							
5							

The above calculation Simplified below.

We are trying to understand how much margin we make by achieving the Sales Targets. Will it be adequate or do we need to Sell more?

Example :

Sell Rate of Product C is = 1100

OP Margin % = 45.55

OP Margin in Amount = 500

Annual Sales Target =1000 Units

Annual Projection (Based on Targets)

Turnover = 1000 * 1100 = 1100000

Margin = 1000 * 500 = 500000

Monthly Projection (Annual Target / 12 = 83 Units)

Turnover = 83 * 1100 = 91300

Margin = 83 * 500 = 41500

Therefore, the Company will earn a Gross Margin of 41500 each Month if the Sales Target of 83 Units is being achieved with respect to Product C.

Similar you need to Create this type of a Projection Chart for all the products and Services.

Post this, you can arrive at Net Profits after deducting your Expenses from the Operational Margin Chart.

The BOSP Thumb Rule :

Step 1 : You Calculated SMET (Simplified Monthly Expenses Tracker)

Step 2 : You Calculated Operational Gain Per Month as per Sales Targets

Projected Operational Gain Per Month should be Higher than SMET. If not, we are currently on a Sinking Ship.

(Don't lose heart. Work on your Targets and see how much do you need to Sell to increase the Projected Gross Earnings)

Sounds like a Plan?

That's why I called it *"Business Operational Success Plan."*

50 PURPOSE OF EXISTENCE

Have you ever wondered what the very Purpose of Existence for your business is? As I have shared earlier, you have a market in your hand as long as you are solving problems.

To spend more time exploring this, you need to make a chart for your Product Offering.

POA - Product Offering Analysis			
Category	**Name of the Product / Service**	**What Solution does it Provide?**	**What are the Pain Points does it Address?**
Cat A	Product 1		
	Product 2		
	Product 3		
	Product 4		
	Product 5		
Cat B	Product 1		
	Product 2		
	Product 3		
	Product 4		
	Product 5		

What Problems are you solving?

What more problems would you like to solve?

** Answering the above will let you define *"Why are you running this Business?"*

HR SYSTEMS

51 AUTOMATE HIRING AND FIRING

Business leaders sometimes get stuck with emotional hiring and emotional firing.

Sounds bizarre? Actually, they do.

Growing companies need to put in a lot of time in building systems that will help them scale-up in all areas.

Questions to Ponder:

- ✓ Do you have a set of clear cut criteria as to what to look for when you hire people?

- ✓ Do you have a set of guidelines to remove people from the system after a prolonged period of poor performance?

Most companies don't have these systems – Because they make this process so emotional. It is essential to love your employees and treat them as your assets. But don't make hiring, firing, salary hikes and promotions an emotional process. Instead set clear guidelines and expectations that will indicate you when to take action on those matters.

** Time for Automation Flow Charts!

HR Automation - Sample:

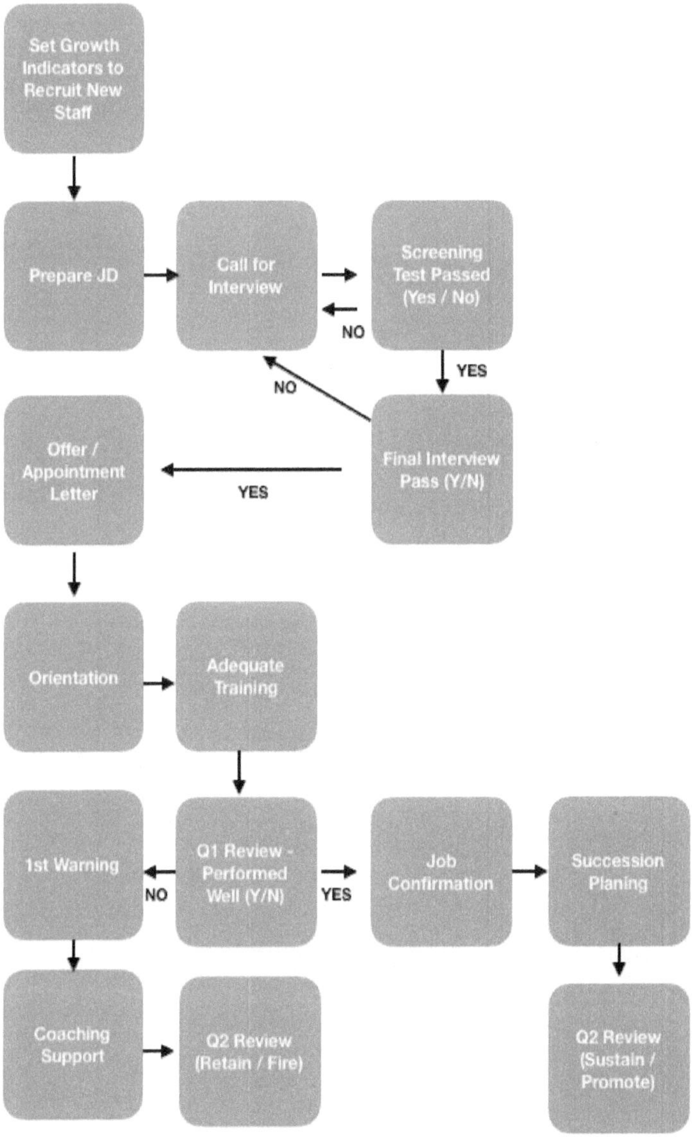

52 JD'S TO BE TEMPLATED FOR YOUR NEED

We all know JD stands for Job Description. In growing companies, what they expect from an employee changes from time to time as they are entirely in the evolving state. However, it is essential to keep your JDs updated for each role.

What information to Cover?

- ✓ Nature of Job
- ✓ Work Timings
- ✓ Reporting to . . .
- ✓ Skills Required & Expected
- ✓ Requirement of Prior Experience
- ✓ Educational Qualifications
- ✓ Demographic Requirement if any
- ✓ Salary Offered
- ✓ Future Growth

** Get this document ready for each and every role / position in your organization. Role clarity is the key to enhanced productivity.

** JDs are mostly used while posting details about job openings. Once people join your team, you then give them a more elaborated and detailed document, and we can call it Roles and Responsibilities document.

53 CREATE YOUR ONBOARDING STYLE

As a business leader, flight journey should be common for you. The crew does not bother whether you are flying for the first time or for the 100th time. They will still orient you – They have their way of Onboarding!

If it is followed rigorously even for a 45 minutes' flight, then think about the onboarding experience you have to provide for your new recruits who will be traveling with your organization for many years to come.

If you don't give a WOW experience on day 1, chances are high - your new recruit will take your company and roles so lightly. It would then be difficult to bring excitement and involvement.

** Make a Checklist for Onboarding Experience

If you are a super busy CEO who travels often, I recommend that you can record a welcome message for your new recruits and it can be played as part of their onboarding experience. (Leverage Everything –Yeah).

Not to miss – Company's Vision, Core Values, HR Policies, Business Policies, Benefits, etc. to be briefed.

Well, you better work on that checklist Now ☺

54 YOU WON'T GROW WITHOUT KPI'S

In growth oriented organizations, clear-cut KPIs (Key Performance Indicators) are designed for their employees. Never underestimate the power of measuring and reviewing the KPIs of your team members periodically.

People can get ambiguous with their deliverables in small and medium companies as they will be doing a whole lot of new things for the betterment of the company.

However, as business leaders, you should never forget their Key Area of Result that will be monitored and reviewed for their promotions, salary revisions, etc.

And remember to Play the Numbers Game - Do not have adjectives part of the KPIs. Make it purely numbers.

Escape Mechanisms:

When KPIs are not clear, your employees will be super busy doing many things, but when you look at the outcomes or measurable results, you will be wondering what they were doing all along.

Taking responsibility is great. That's when leaders evolve. But not at the cost of forgetting their KPIs or not fulfilling them.

** Define KPIs for each and every person in your core team. Review this for over three months and then let them define KPIs for people reporting to them.

Have all the reports centralized, so you are monitoring it.
(Auto-Pilot Mode)

55 GAMIFY YOUR BUSINESS

Performance Acceleration through Gamification!

The human brain is wired to compete, win and celebrate victory. From the childhood days, we have all enjoyed games and competitions.

In today's scenario, it is essential to create a platform where employees can perform and showcase their talents through unique competitions. (Human mind craves to step into new avenues without the fear of failing)

The performance gamification is a new trend in HRM that enables employees to deliver their best in line with their KPIs in sync with the organization's values.

Sounds interesting?

Well, you just need to set points and slabs for each KPI. Based on the Performance, you can arrive at a percentage of points scored!

70% and Above – Great Performance

50% and Above – Average Performance

< than 50% - Poor Performance

Gamification can be done for Individuals, Teams, Departments, and Divisions.

Tip: Setting a good rewards system is very important for the winners. When you roll this out, your people may think *"What is in it for me?"*.

Sales KPI - Gamified - Sample: (Individual Performance)

Performance Metrics - SALES		
Area	**Points**	**Details**
Attendance	10	1st Leave: 8 Points 2nd Leave: 5 Points
Timing	10	1 Late : 8 Points 2 Lates: 5 Points
KPI - 1	20	Total Sales Volume Target: XX Lakhs (Pro Rata Basis) Points = Achieved/Target*100
KPI - 2	20	Fresh Sales Volume (New Clients) Target: XX Lakhs (Pro Rata Basis) Points = Achieved/Target*100
KPI - 3	20	Generate New Leads Target: 200 (Pro Rata Basis) Points = Achieved/Target*100
KPI - 4	10	Get Video Testimonials 2 Testimonials 5 Pts Per Testimonial
Daily Reports	10	Submitted: 10 Points
	100	

56 HIRE FOR ATTITUDE

Are you hiring based on skills and knowledge? You are doing a wise thing. But there is a much wiser thing you can do!

If people join your organization and shouldn't leave forever, how would you hand pick?

Yes, I am talking about attitude – What one thinks of themselves, their core beliefs, mindset and more. That doesn't mean you only look for these attributes in a person when you recruit them. Of course, skill and knowledge are essential.

But I want you to keep one thing in mind.

Skills can be trained
Knowledge can be imparted
Attitude has to come from within.

It's a challenge to Transform and change a person's Mind-Set, and Psychologists like me work on such behavioural modifications.

However, the point here is simple. Look for both and let attitude be given the highest level of importance.

** List out what attitude and behavioural patterns you are looking for concerning each role and department in your Organization.

57 TESTING AFTER HIRING IS A FAILURE

I just shared that attitude is to be given the utmost importance when you recruit a person. The second most important thing you look at is skills and knowledge.

Don't forget this word *"Billability."* This lets you take the decision on what salary you can offer to the new recruit. Can they kick-start work from day 1 or week 1 and be a billable resource? – Generating revenue for the company.

The most common mistake business leaders do is, they have an oral conversation with the candidate and assume that they are Pro level in skills and technical areas.

Action Item:

- ✓ Set clear assessments to be carried out for each JD.
- ✓ Come up with a rating system for the results
- ✓ Put this into practice

Help Needed?:

For the initial screening, if you are looking to conduct "Verbal, General Knowledge and Analytical based assessments," do reach out to us and our team will mail you three sets of questions and answer keys - you can mix, match and use them.

Mail us at business@revelationconsulting.in with a brief introduction of your Business.

BUSINESS INTELLIGENCE

58 LEADERS WILL HAVE DASHBOARDS

It's time for Business Dashboards. All your significant numbers such as sales, products, purchase, payments, profits, and every other key aspect with target vs. percentage of achievement chart will become your customized Business Dashboard.

Make it look super cool, trendy and colorful. Let this Dashboard take the central place in your desktop or office wall.

Still Wondering how it can be that Peppy?

- ✓ Have a look at your website analytics report
- ✓ Have a look at your Social Media Page analytics report
- ✓ They are Super Colourful
- ✓ Every Single Detail is Captured
- ✓ Last month to current month growth and decline areas are Highlighted
- ✓ Motivates you to pay more attention to look at it
- ✓ The more regularly you look at it, the better you become at understanding it.

** Dear CEO, it's time for Business Dashboard.
Be a Super Boss!

59 MAKE YOUR WEBSITE YOUR FRONT OFFICE

Is your website generating you Leads?

Well, that's your digital front office. People spend so much money on the interiors of their home and offices. A great couch, welcome lounge, curtains, coffee table and much more. What about keeping your digital front office that attractive?

There are no holidays for your website. It works for your Business 24/7 projecting the best of your services and offering to generate leads.

Undoubtedly one of the best investments for any Business is to have a world-class website. Most businesses fail to keep their website up to date with the latest testimonials, updates, offerings, new initiatives, and blogs.

Blogs can be educating articles related to your business. Publish a blog every week, share it on social media and see how organic traffic improves on your website.

** Time for Website Audit!

Best Layout for a Professional website

- Home - About Us
- Offering / Services
- Vision
- Core Values
- USP / Why Choose Us
- Testimonials
- Management
- Awards / Accreditations
- Careers / Grow with us
- Contact Us - Contact Form, Maps, Social Media

Tip :

Have a Newsletter sign up column to build your E-Mail list.

(If need be, offer an excellent educating article for free where people can sign up and download or receive it in their mailbox).

60 FOCUS LIKE EAGLE

An eagle can spot its prey even at a distance of 3.2 Km. That's FOCUS!

Businesses don't grow when the core leaders are scattered and not focused on the Results.

People tend to get excited with the flow of things and lose focus eventually. Business leaders need to keep aligning the team periodically towards results – Traction matters!

You should also be familiar with the saying *"You can't chase two rabbits at the same time."* Though there are a few sets of Goals to be achieved both in the short run as well as long run, as business leaders, keep your Eagle-Eyed Focus on the one thing that is most important and let it drive you every single day.

Similarly – your core team leaders are to be lead and influenced by the single most important goal to work on with Eagle-Eyed Focus.

** Start writing the one Thing that should matter for Each Division.

61 COST ANALYSIS IS THE KEY FOR PROFITS

Business Goals – solve problems – create good will & make profits. You are not going to make profits only by increasing your sales. You need to look at the cost metrics.

Businesses don't make profits when their cost analysis is not done. It's like filling water in a leaky bucket. When was the last time you did cost accounting for your Business? – Basically accounting each and every expense to a particular product/service / process to arrive at the exact cost.

In fact, cost analysis should be one of the main factors (apart from competitor analysis) in fixing a price for a product / service.

Here are some of the interesting facts you will find when you do Cost Analysis.

- ✓ What are the most profitable products / services?
- ✓ What are the loss-making products / services?
- ✓ What are the top 5 Costs that are increasing your selling price?
- ✓ What percentage of the turnover and profits are your spending on salaries?

** Time for Cost Accounting in your Business

62 INTERPRET BALANCE SHEETS OR CUSTOM CREATE THEM

As business leaders, we must build the skill of interpreting balance sheets. Well, there could be certain words or concepts which may confuse you initially – But mastering this will help you to stay on top of the game.

We always have another option!

Interpreting balance sheets doesn't excite you, or it seems to be a tough thing to crack? no worries. Just custom create a basic template in which you want the reports each month.

This can also be the back-end data of your business dashboard we talked about earlier! Just look at all the significant numbers that need to be tracked for your business and find a way to review them in a way you understand.

Tip:

When things don't go well, looking at these numbers may get you tensed and lose your cool. Chill, relax, take a deep breath and look carefully into the numbers because your breakthrough is also waiting there!

Remember to celebrate your breakdowns.

And when you are on cloud nine due to massive success, don't miss to look into what gave you this Victory.

63 PAYMENTS AND EXCITEMENTS

When the money hits the bank account, it creates an excitement that gives hope for many things to come.

When does a wise entrepreneur get excited? Here are different stages when people get excited.

(Here excited is referred to not just that happy feeling. But getting ready to spend your next buck – increase expenses – invest more – take a big leap)

- ✓ When the new inquiry reaches
- ✓ After sending the proposal
- ✓ Once the PO is released / Order confirmed
- ✓ After dispatch
- ✓ After getting the payments

Now, you should be thinking. "A wise entrepreneur should spend more / increase the expenses / spend the next buck only after getting the payments.

Not really – That's not enough. It is when

- ✓ You have calculated your operational margins
- ✓ Settled the cost expenses to the vendors
- ✓ Now look at the gross revenue
- ✓ If at all you have profits left over, you can spend further.

This is how a wise Entrepreneur works. Trust me on this. This way you will reduce unnecessary expenses, bring financial discipline and fasten your way to making big profits.

(When you want to expand, invest or borrow, that is a different scenario. But practice this hack to the fullest).

CULTURE

64 CREATE VALUES FOR WORK & LIFE

What is the Culture of your organization?

Some business owners have not really thought about this question.

How does the Organization Culture / Climate gets formed?

It all starts with a set of Core Belief systems that people practice.

On that note, you can create a culture for your organization by creating, following and practicing a set of core values. *Organizational Values are best observed when people consider them as Personal Life Values too!*

Sample - core values for Save The Globe (Our NGO)

Live, Love and Look. . .

- Live by your Word
  (Keep up Commitments)

- Love People for who they are
  (Accept People the way they are)

- Look for Opportunities in every Obstacle
  (Never Give Up)

** List down 30 words that will define the value systems of your organization. Then run a brainstorming session with your core team to create organization values.

65 COACH PEOPLE WITH VALUES

The Core Values are not something that is just printed and framed on the walls of your company. That needs to be the DNA of your people's belief system.

When they have taken it as values for their own life, this brings a culture change and a mindset shift.

During breakdowns or issues, you don't have to burn yourself too much correcting people. All you have to do is to get to the coaching mode to see what values are missing.

Example:

Say one of your Core Values is *"Treat People with Respect."* Two employees are having tough conversations and using foul language on each other.

You don't have to get into the scene and give them a long lecture about handling conflicts. Just play the Coach role and tell them . . .

- ✓ Can you understand that one of our Core Values is to *"Treat People with Respect"?*
- ✓ Can you understand you are *not living the Values and bringing down the morale of our Team?*
- ✓ What needs to happen for you to *"Treat each other with Respect"?*

** Core Values.
Really builds a Great Organizational Culture

66 CELEBRATING THE DIFFERENCE OF OPINION

How beautiful would it be if there are no arguments and misunderstandings within the team? Well, some employees may prefer to have a team like that.

If you find a team who has no quarrel whatsoever, then chances are high that they are masking it. As business leaders, you need to educate your team to have open and honest Conversations. *The fear of what the other person will think of me - is a virus at the workplace.*

Let these thoughts sink in.

- ✓ Misunderstanding leads to better understanding.
- ✓ The team that argues together works together.
- ✓ The team that fights together stays together.
- ✓ The team that voices out work with full involvement.
- ✓ Real teams do not act with a being-nice mask. They practice being themselves and accept each other for who they are.

** Now you got a PEP talk to give to your Team!

67 HACK GROWTH WITH SHARED ACCOUNTABILITY

Accountability is the best word that must be used and practiced in every organization. In pure form, it is to ensure people are on track to fulfill their commitments.

In companies where growth doesn't happen – everyone thinks only the Team Lead / Head / Boss can hold others accountable to ensure they are doing their part thoroughly in achieving the overall Goal.

They think it is none of their business to poke into someone else's work, even if they know something is not right with it or it is causing damage to the organization's growth. This needs to change.

Educate your people to hold each other accountable. This is not about bossing around and pushing people. It can be practiced gently by asking

- ✓ How can I help you today?
- ✓ How can I help you to reach your Goals?
- ✓ I am on track to finish my tasks. Are you? Need help?

68 PLAY THE HOT SEAT GAME ONCE A QUARTER

This is my personal favorite. I have run this initiative for many of my clients and has been a super hit everywhere.

I suggest every growth oriented company does this once in 6 months!

Let's dive into the process:

Step 1 – Everyone assemble together (Do this first with your core team). Circled seating is better, and classroom seating is also fine.

Venue : At your own Office / Resort / Camp Fire.

Step 2 – Get the first person to sit on the Hot Seat. (Go with random order or use lot method)

Step 3 – Everyone now shares positive inputs about that person. Edification time. Encourage people to look at their eyes and appreciate face to face. Encourage everyone to share – What goes around comes around.

Step 4 – Now it's time for Feedforwards. It is to basically tell them the areas of improvement on a positive note. Things that they can do better in the future.

At this point – It is mandatory for the person sitting on the Hot Seat to write down those Feedforwards. That's how we show respect for such valuable inputs.

Also, encourage everyone to share. Teach them - sharing these inputs does not mean putting others down. It is the best way to show that you are committed to their betterment.

Bonus Point: Whoever is sitting on the Hot Spot should also be gently told – That after 6 Months when we sit here for another Hot Seat program, they should not be getting the same feedforwards. That would mean they are taking this team for granted and not committed for personal excellence.

And the person sitting on the Hot Seat should take this as others' point of view. The inputs they receive should not be ignored completely or even taken too seriously. It is wise to listen with an open mind, not respond back or retaliate with feedforwards and instead process them in their mind as to how these inputs can make their lives better! The team that argues together grows together.

Step 5 – Time for the next person. Repeat from step 3 till you are done with the last person.

Tips:

- ✓ Set timer to stay on track.
- ✓ Stick to the point.
- ✓ Do not repeat what others have said.
- ✓ At least once in a Year – Business Owners also must sit and go through this process. Trust me, this will be the most significant gift you can give your employees. They will trust you at a whole new level.

** Have your first Hot Seat Program this month!

OPERATIONAL SYSTEMS

69 BELIEVE THAT SOP'S ARE RESOURCE SAVERS

SOP – Standard Operating Procedure.

All major Department Activities are to be defined with SOPs. Well, this may look like a tedious process. But you have great leverage on this.

To run your business in Auto-Pilot Mode, you need to set the SOPs in place. This will save you a lot of time. People will not be pestering you for repeated silly queries. They just have to go by the operational policies.

As and when new situations arise, you can always update the SOPs. This eventually will contribute towards productivity habits where people say *"In our Organization, this is how things are done."*

SOP – Benefits:

- ✓ Man Power utilized Efficiently (Error repetition avoided)
- ✓ Raw Materials used Optimally (Wastage Reduced)
- ✓ Money Managed well (Low Wastages and High Productivity)
- ✓ Machines utilized optimally
- ✓ Time is used Efficiently
- ✓ Energy is Saved (Electricity, Avoiding Repeated Work)

70 THERE ARE NO EMERGENCY TASKS

Emergency tasks will steal the show. It can even kill a whole day's productivity. When I say – There is no emergency tasks, I am not telling you to ignore such things but to get to the root of the cause.

Root Cause:

There are *"Routine Tasks"* that should be created and followed rigorously. It needs to be given importance as per the execution routine created. Consider that when you miss fulfilling a routine task, it eventually grows up to become an emergency task.

When that happens, it not only steals your time and attention but also spoils few other routine tasks. And later those routine tasks will grow up to become emergency tasks. This is again a sabotaging cycle.

From personal life to business environment, there can be routine tasks created and executed. This will enable you to do more in less time, avoid last-minute stress and run your business in Auto-Pilot Mode.

Honestly, think about it.

If a machine is maintained periodically, it won't cause unnecessary breakdowns due to poor maintenance. You will save man power, avoid productivity loss and even save the opportunity cost.

Make a list of routines and tasks that can be created and set for each Department.

Routine Tasks

- ✓ Things to be Done
    - o Daily
    - o Weekly
    - o Bi-Weekly
    - o Monthly
    - o Bi-Monthly
    - o Quarterly
    - o Bi-Annually
    - o Annually

- ✓ Special Routines like 1st Monday or 3rd Wednesday

Some Random Things that we miss out!

- ✓ Routine
    - o To take Back up of Business Files
    - o To Maintain Air Conditioners
    - o To Check UPS and Batteries
    - o For Pest Control
    - o For Mobile Back Up
    - o For New Blog Release
    - o For Digital Newsletters
    - o To File Arrangements
    - o For Outstation Visits

The list is huge.

** Start framing these Routines for your Business!

71 BANK ON CUSTOMER FEEDBACK

Now, do you have a routine to collect customer feedbacks?

- ✓ Feedback within 1st Week of doing Business
- ✓ Feedback within 1st Week of Losing an Order
- ✓ Bi-Annual or Annual Feedback – General Opinion, Suggestions, Expectations, etc.

Several insights are waiting for the growth of your business with these feedbacks. Never ever take them lightly. Nothing like getting inputs from your most valuable customers who really wish you growth and expansion.

Step 1 – Create a routine for feedbacks to be received.

Step 2 – Set easy questions for each feedback routine.

Step 3 – Choose the right medium to receive feedback.

- ✓ It can be an SMS – along with a link that lands on a Digital Form
- ✓ It can be an E-Mail sent along with a Digital Form
- ✓ It can be over a Call from your Office
- ✓ If can be over a Physical Mail

Step 4 – Start Today!

GROWTH ASPECTS

72 EXPANSION ANALYSIS

Businesses are meant to soar new heights. Entrepreneurs should keep thinking about the Next Level and Expansion!

First, Business Expansion happens in your Mindset and next it happens in reality.

Things to consider when you are planning on expansion!

- ✓ Own Expansion or Franchise Model?
- ✓ Own Manufacturing or Outsourced Model?
- ✓ Market Study and Survey
- ✓ Demographics from Social Media Platforms
- ✓ Competitor Analysis
- ✓ SWOT
- ✓ Market Potential
- ✓ Competitor Market Share
- ✓ Untapped Markets
- ✓ Alternative Products and Services
- ✓ Pricing Strategy for New Markets
- ✓ Fund Raising
- ✓ Investor Pitch and Proposal
- ✓ Return On Investment
- ✓ Exit Strategy – Getting ready for the Worst
- ✓ Organic Growth – Self Sufficient Funding

** Expansion Mode - On

73 LET CLC DO THE MAGIC

Employees want growth. They like to reach the next Level in their Careers. How many designations can you offer for your employees?

If you look deep enough, you will realize we may be able to offer two or maximum three designations for an employee in their lifetime. Even that would be challenging for certain roles.

And that is why we have invented CLC for you – *Career Ladder Chart.* We have implemented this for our clients, and the results were so amazing that employees felt like contributing and growing with the company forever.

What's the problem with the regular model?

Let's take the case of an Office that has only one Receptionist.

Can you call them as:

Receptionist
Sr. Receptionist
Super Senior Receptionist
Manager Receptionist?

Sounds funny right?

Well, this can be better. Let me show you how.

CLC – Create about 5 different grading and growth levels for your company. This can be for overall organization or department wise as preferred.

At each level, there can be clear eligibility criteria and benefits given for the employees.

Illustration:

Company Name: ABC Ltd

The five CLS Levels can be termed with letters from the Company Name.

AB – 1

Eligibility:
Finish Probation Period
Score 70+ Points in Gamification Metrics

Benefits:
Monthly One Paid Leave
Annual Bonus

AB – 2

Eligibility:
Take up a New Challenge and Bring it to Results in 60 Days
Mentor a New Intern and Make them Perform in KPIs

Benefits:
All Benefits of AB – 1
Annual Local Family Tour Voucher Worth XXX

AB – 3

Eligibility:
Set One New Record in the Hall of Fame

Benefits:
All Benefits of AB - 2
International Family Tour Voucher

AB – 4

Eligibility:
To be defined

Benefits:
To be defined
Ideas – Annual Scholarship for Children's Education

AB – 5

Eligibility:
To be defined

Benefits:
To be defined
Ideas – 0.5% share from Company's Annual Profits

** The above inputs given are basic. You need to spend more time to come up with 5 CLC levels for your company that will create that WOW feeling for your employees. This is an excellent way to give them hope for the future and communicate how much you value them!

74 BUSINESS CALENDAR

Well planned is half done. When other important events are clashing with your personal events and dates, you feel disturbed right?

You get this thought – *"Had I known this earlier, I would have planned things better."* One of the best gifts you can give your business as well as employees is a one year calendar in advance.

Jot down all the significant events that need to be scheduled such as

- ✓ Quarterly Review Dates
- ✓ Training Dates
- ✓ Annual Celebration
- ✓ Awards Night
- ✓ Dealers Meeting
- ✓ Exhibitions

1 – You can set an automated count down for each of the events along with their checklist and deadlines, so things begin to fall in place. (Routine Task vs. Emergency Task)

2 – Your Employees can plan their personal calendar accordingly. At the core of their hearts, they don't want to take vacations at the cost of company's growth. Most of the time these two schedules clash purely as a coincidence. Then you say No – Their family is not happy with the work and blah blah blah.

Just release your calendar. (Unplanned emergencies both in business and family cannot be avoided. But other things can perfectly fall into place. Start Today!)

75 AWARDS NIGHT

As a growing organization, it is vital for us to connect with our employees on a personal level. The Awards Night perfectly makes way for it to happen.

To Dos for Awards Night:

- ✓ Make it an Evening Event – Set the dates in advance
- ✓ Invite your Employees with their Family Members (This is a great morale booster).
- ✓ Plan for the Programs – You will be surprised how much talent your people have got – Singing, Dancing, Best Couple Event, Fun Games and more.
- ✓ Make a Year Review Video, Share Vision, Share Next Year Growth Plans.
- ✓ Give Awards for the Top Performers.

Some Award Categories

- ✓ Highest Sales / Dispatch / Customer Ratings, Etc
- ✓ Individual Performers and Team Awards
- ✓ Hall of Fame Winners – Setting All-time High Records
- ✓ Fun - Most Well Dressed, Most Stylish, Most Techie Person

** You are for sure fixing up the date for your First Awards Night Event.

76 LEGROMA

This is a tool we suggest every company should implement irrespective of whether they are small or big.

LeGroMa stands for *Learning Growth Map*. Just like how we had the CLC levels for growth in the organization, we need to create Learning Growth Map for each department and make it customized for every employee.

Process:

- ✓ Run a Skill Competency Assessment for Employees
- ✓ Skills Needed vs. Current Skills Score (You may need an expert's guidance in arriving at these Metrics)
- ✓ Based on their Current Skill Level, Exposure and Experience, they should be able to Choose different Learning Programs offered to them through the Company (In-House Training or other Special Programs)
- ✓ Set Results Expected and Milestones for each Person.
- ✓ Set up Points / Credits System for the progress and Gamify the Learning too.
- ✓ They now know their next level of Growth. What needs to be Achieved is clear, and the Resources are accessible to them as well.

77 SSG & BTG

Goals, Goals, Goals. . . We have targets in every division at our office. I want you to recollect what we learned with the BOSP concept – Business Operational Success Plan. You need to know what are the margins and the gain revenue from your sales. Now I am connecting back to that through SSG and BTG.

SSG – Sure Shot Goal
BTG – Breakthrough Goal

Well, this is not the concept of aim for the Breakthrough Goal, and you will reach your Sure Shot Goal. Nope. They are different.

SSG – Sure Shot Goal – Based on the Growth rate your business needs to achieve, you set this Goal. Most importantly this Goal should give you enough Operational Margins to take care of your Needed Expenses. You are growing, not in a loss, but profits are increasing gradually.

BTG – Breakthrough Goals – You want to Scale your Business to the best of its potential. You are looking at a total trajectory shift in the way your business is growing. This Goal should give you enough Operational Margins to even take care of your Desired Expenses. Creating Wealth, Financial Stability and Happiness for you and your Team. You are Soaring New Heights, skimming the best of profits and experiencing rapid growth.

** What is your SSG and BTG this Year?

REVENUE GENERATORS

78 THE BUSINESS PITCH

Who is the Brand Ambassador for your organization?

For a growing concern, I must say all your employees are your Brand Ambassadors.

Business owners and sales professionals eventually get better at giving a business pitch. That's because it's a part of their job and without a proper business pitch they can't get appointments to meet with the top people in the City. (At times even business owners and sales professionals miss to create an inspiring business pitch)

However, it is essential to educate, orient and train your entire team with a business pitch (An excellent and inspiring way of introducing your company). This helps in morale-boosting as well as creating a highly respectable brand image for your organization in the society.

Illustration:

A Person works in a Coffee Shop

The Usual Intro – (5 Secs):

Hi, I am working in a Coffee shop that is located near the city library.

Inspiring Intro – (15 Secs):

Hi, my name is Ken, and I am representing ABC Coffee Spot.

- ✓ Each Day we Serve 100 New Customers
- ✓ Awarded "No.1 Customer's Choice" by XYZ Magazine
- ✓ We use Home Grown Coffee Bean and support local farmers.

** Script your Business Intro – Let your people get better at introducing your organization like a Pro.

The task for your Sales Team:

While everyone in your organization has a good intro pitch, your sales and marketing team (Including CXOs) should have different pitches for different people they meet.

Think of this like Bowling in Cricket! There are different styles of Bowling, and we use it accordingly based on the Batsman and the Pitch. CXOs need to know multiple ways of introducing their business based on the place and the person they are interacting with.

79 SALES + VISUALS

What influences a customer to take their wallet out and give you that money / swipe their card and complete the purchase?

There are a whole number of factors. Price, model, sales person, influencing friend and the list goes on. Three major things needs to be focused and integrated with sales process to boost the chances of buying.

The first would be Visuals – There are two parts for Visuals – What the Customer sees and what they imagine. Both need to be tapped in positively for better conversion.

The see and imagine elements:

- ✓ Brochure
- ✓ Product Itself
- ✓ Attractive Display and Shelving
- ✓ Creative Designs with Customer Testimonials
- ✓ Getting a thought of how this product would positively impact their lives

** List out some of the Specific Visuals to be added and incorporated in your Sales Process.

It's Time for a Positive influence.

80 SALES + RIGHT WORDS

The second influencing factor in making the customer buy the products is the usage of the right words. This may sound more like a simple thing but makes a world of difference.

We are influenced by what we hear. What goes inside can keep ringing, again and again, making the customers to even come back to buy what they inquired earlier.

Some Words for you to get an Idea:

- ✓ This suits you the Most
- ✓ Rare and Unique Product / Collection
- ✓ Fast Moving
- ✓ Just Arrived
- ✓ This is Now in Trend
- ✓ Looks like Made for you
- ✓ ROI . . . XY Months
- ✓ Double your . . . .
- ✓ Reduce your . . . . . by XY %

** List out some of the Specific Words to be added and incorporated in your Sales Process.

81 SALES + TOUCH & FEEL

We need to make buying from us a unique experience. The third ingredient that creates an amazing buying experience is touch and feel.

Customers love to touch and feel our products as they buy from us. In some instances such as service sectors, touch and feel could be a challenge.

For instance, I am a Business Coach, and I can provide the touch and feel experience through – Writing a book like this, offer webinars and share video testimonials.

An Insurance Company can do this with – Brochures, Making the prospect talk to another client who is also a beneficiary, share video testimonials, honor the client by being on time, send monthly newsletters and more.

Some Touch Feel Factors:

- ✓ Product Trial
- ✓ Free Trial – Limited Period Offer
- ✓ Gift Vouchers
- ✓ Live Demo
- ✓ Sample Pack
- ✓ Client Onboarding Experience

** List out some of the Specific Touch& Feel factors to be added and incorporated in your Sales Process.

82 BELIEVE IN THE PREMIUM MARKET

In a way, many businesses are part of the Rat Race. There is a market, and it is flooded with lot of competitors. Yes, we can't avoid competition. But we can provide the best services possible in a way that customers' pain points are addressed.

With all the struggling and hustling in the rat race, we fail to consider that there is a market out there for the Premium and elite crowd. Mostly it is not crowded – There are very few players out there sharing the major chunk of the Premium Business in the market.

This is not about stopping what you are doing and focusing only on the premium segment. No – let your breadwinner keep running successfully as it is now. But parallel to that, see how you can roll out a Premium Product or Service in the market and let it grow. It will not clash your current growth because the consumers for both markets are mostly different.

Premium Segment:

- ✓ People who are willing to pay any price for the Quality they want.
- ✓ People who put convenience first and cost next.
- ✓ People who cannot put up with poor quality
- ✓ People who prefer everything in one place – Ease of Access
- ✓ People with bad experiences with Competitors and Cheap Products or Services

** Start working on your Premium Product!

83 CONTACTS ARE YOUR ASSETS

Depending on the number of years you are in Business, you would have earned contacts – Customers, Prospects and Vendors.

Would you do a simple calculation for me today?

- ✓ Calculate the Total Salary Expenses Per Month
- ✓ Calculate the Total Over Heads Per Month (Rent, Bills, Etc)
- ✓ Grand Total (Salary + Overheads)
- ✓ Calculate the Average number of New Contacts you get each Month (Inquiries, New Connections gained through your Sales Team)
- ✓ Value Per Contact = (New Contacts / Total Expenses)

When you look at how much you are spending per contact, you will start cherishing them and giving them the utmost importance.

To Do :

- ✓ Create a Central Database of Contacts for easy Access.
- ✓ Create a System such that every New contact generated should be added to the database the same day.
- ✓ Create a System where these contacts are being engaged (E-Mail Automation / Newsletters and more)

** Repeatedly teach your team that Contacts are assets.

HABITUAL SUCCESS

84 MEETING ROUTINES - VAT

Some Companies burn huge number of hours with meetings. At times people even lose focus in these meetings and end up discussing entirely different issues.

Why Meetings become Boring?

- ✓ No Clear Agenda
- ✓ Do not Start and End on Time
- ✓ Action Items are not Noted
- ✓ Not following up Previous Meeting's Discussion
- ✓ End up discussing different Issues

How Meetings Need to be?

- ✓ Pre-Fixed – Routine Set - Automated
- ✓ Have a Clear Agenda – Shared Prior to Meeting
- ✓ Start and End on Time
- ✓ Note down Action Items, Deadline
- ✓ Set Accountability for Action Items
- ✓ Important Issues should be Addressed
- ✓ Solutions and Decision to be taken (Decide in the Meeting. Regarding major decisions, the point person can later check with the Authorities and revert with the final call)
- ✓ Mistakes done should not be hidden

We have come up with VAT format of Meetings to ensure Fast Track Growth is accelerated.

- ✓ Vision Meeting
- ✓ Action Meeting
- ✓ Task Meeting

85 VISION MEETINGS

VAT Meetings will enable you to play the Coach role in the best possible way for your team. It will equip you to stay on top of the game.

Vision Meeting:

- ✓ Happens Monthly Once
- ✓ Ideal Duration – Half a Day
  (Once in three months, make it a full day by running a Half Day Learning Program- In-House or Outsourced)
- ✓ Looking at Last Month Performance
- ✓ Compare it with Annual Targets
- ✓ Discussions with Created Business Dashboard
- ✓ SSG Review
- ✓ BTG Review
- ✓ KPIs Review
- ✓ Major Hits and Misses are Discussed
- ✓ Learning from Breakdowns
- ✓ Feedforwards within the Core Team
- ✓ Learning session based on Skill Gap and Performance Lag
- ✓ CXOs MUST be a part of this – If you miss this meeting, you are missing to hold the steering of your Ship!

** It's time to add VAT Meetings to your Annual Business Calendar.

Vision Meeting Template:

<table>
<tr><th colspan="5">VAT - Vision & Strategy Meeting</th></tr>
<tr><td>Team Name:</td><td></td><td rowspan="2">VAT Format</td><td>Chair Person:</td><td></td></tr>
<tr><td>Date & Venue</td><td>Monthly</td><td>Meeting Duration:</td><td>One Day / Half Day based on Lead / Lag Level</td></tr>
<tr><th colspan="5">Meeting Purpose</th></tr>
<tr><td colspan="5">Previous Month Review</td></tr>
<tr><td colspan="5">Awards, Recognition, Hall of Fame</td></tr>
<tr><td colspan="5">Brainstorming for Current and Upcoming Quarter</td></tr>
<tr><th colspan="5">Meeting Agenda:</th></tr>
<tr><th>Time Duration</th><th>Agenda</th><th>Owner</th><th>Hits & Misses</th><th>Action Items</th></tr>
<tr><td>10 mins</td><td>Achievement of Previous Month</td><td></td><td></td><td></td></tr>
<tr><td>10 mins</td><td>Breakdowns of Previous Month</td><td></td><td></td><td></td></tr>
<tr><td>1 Hr</td><td>Feed Forward Session
Quick Hot Seat Program</td><td></td><td></td><td></td></tr>
<tr><td>10 mins</td><td>Awards / Rewards</td><td></td><td></td><td></td></tr>
<tr><td>1 Hr Max</td><td>Results Targets for Next Month
Action Targets for Next Month
(G = N + D)
Vision Casting</td><td></td><td></td><td></td></tr>
<tr><td>1 Hr Max</td><td>Breakthrough Session:
What's Not Working
Critical Issues
Emotions
Root Cause</td><td></td><td></td><td></td></tr>
<tr><td>2 to 3 Hrs Max</td><td>Learning Session</td><td></td><td></td><td></td></tr>
<tr><td>15 mins</td><td>Close with Reinforcements</td><td></td><td></td><td></td></tr>
</table>

86 ACTION MEETINGS

Businesses miss to Grow also because of slow realization – Analyzing the problem after it is over. To steer Peak Performance, you will need to have a mid-month Alignment Meeting.

I am proposing this VAT model after testing different meeting routines with hundreds of clients and seeing what has really given us good results.

Action Meetings:

- ✓ This is a 15 Day Meeting
- ✓ Ideal Duration: 1.5 Hours
- ✓ (Might be a half day event in case a Mini Learning session is conducted for another 1.5 Hrs – Preferably Technical or Product Related)
- ✓ Mid-Month Alignment
- ✓ Looking at where we are and run a Reality Check
- ✓ Weekly Goals and Tasks should be Reviewed
- ✓ Action Items for the Next two Weeks should be set
- ✓ Critical Issues are Discussed
- ✓ Solutions Brainstormed
- ✓ Close with a PEP Talk

** Start implementing Action Meetings.

In case you need the templates for Action and Task Meetings like how we shared for the Vision Meeting, please mail us at business@revelationconsulting.in with a Brief introduction about your Business.

87 TASK MEETINGS

So we are set with our Monthly Vision Meetings and Bi-Weekly Action Meetings to ensure the team is being proactively Coached for Next Level.

Don't get the thought of – "*WHAT? Yet another meeting?*"

Task meetings are your daily stand up meetings which last only for 10 Minutes. This is where people declare their daily *To Do list* and it must be in sync with their goals. In some instances where the people work remotely and where people report to different locations, this stand-up meeting may not be possible. In such cases, the team members can post their *"To Do list"* for the day in the internal Communication group or application for the company.

Task Meetings:

- ✓ Daily Standup Meetings (As CXO, if you are in town, you can attend this meeting)
- ✓ It is more like a Warm up for the Day.
- ✓ Include "Company's Oath or Common Prayer before the Start" – A superb morale booster.
- ✓ The Top 3 Wins for the Day to be declared by each person.
- ✓ In case they require any Support from others or Management, it can also be mentioned when they Share.
- ✓ Set Timer for 30 Sec to 60 Sec for Each Person – You don't want to burn time in meetings first thing in the morning.
- ✓ Only Sharing Mode and not in Discussion Mode – Any issues and topics that require discussion, concerned people can have a private meeting after the Task Meeting.

88 ACTION TARGET VS RESULT TARGET

Every time we focus on the End Results, we just want each Employee to fulfill their KPIs. As business leaders, if you push people to achieve their Result Targets (End Results) – They may feel pressurized and stuck with proceeding further (unresourceful state – Negative response towards Breakdowns).

By playing the Coach Role, we need to push people towards "Action Target" – Things that are directly within their league, things that they need to be doing to reach the End Results.

Action Target	Results Target
Baby Steps / Process Control	End Results
Within the League	Not Fully within the League
Absolutely our Responsibility	Involves External Environment

Though we need the End Results for Growth, consider the fact that only when you take action, you are going to make progress. Feeling bad that you are not on track is not going to help. Proactively taking actions, trying different things will give you Progress.

Illustration:

John runs a Training and Development Company and here are his Targets for the Month.

Results Target (End Results)

- ✓ Achieve 15 Training Days for the Month
- ✓ Get 5 New Clients
- ✓ Reach XY Revenue in Billing

Each day if he only looks at these Goals, there is not going to be any progress. However, he is accountable for these results. Core Leaders will self-introspect very well and come up with action plans. But not everyone will. That is why Business Leaders like you should play the Coach role in helping people to see what action they can take to reach their Goals.

Action Targets (Things he can do and must do at any cost – within the league)

- ✓ Approach 50 Organizations in the first 5 Days – Sales Calls and Meetings.
- ✓ Roll out a New Program or Theme and send an E-Mail to 1000 Companies – Key Decision Makers in the first week.
- ✓ Talk to 30 other Clients who have stopped giving business in recent times.
- ✓ Release a Promo Video (Mini Training Module)
- ✓ Run a Social Media Campaign
- ✓ Release three Blogs in the first three Weeks
- ✓ Get 3 Video Testimonials from old clients.

** The list can go on . . .

HOLISTIC GOAL SETTING

89 HOLISTIC GOALS FOR EVERYONE

From a psychological standpoint of view, I use to wonder why people don't achieve their goals at office / why they take it lightly / why they feel they are being pushed.

After analyzing this with thousands of people I realized, what is inside shows up outside too. In a sense, people who do not have clear personal goals are not taking the business goals seriously.

When they look at their personal life, personal growth, health, wealth and other areas, there are not big goals that pushes them from within. The only place in their life where they have goals, review systems and being held accountable is office.

Note: Not every employee falls into this category. But this is something we need to be aware to ensure that we have self-driven Leaders as Employees.

What Next?

- ✓ They need to set specific and measurable Goals in all areas of their Lives
- ✓ G = N + D (Goals should be in Number and have a Deadline)
- ✓ Focus on Holistic Goals – Whole Person Concept – They need to be Achievers and Doers in all areas (The 7F Goals) – Future, Family, Friends, Fitness, Fun, Finance, Focus + Faith

90 FUTURE GOALS

As business leaders, we can hold our team accountable for their Personal Goals. Support them by way of Coaching and Mentoring them to set their Goals every year in all the 7 areas of Life.

An employee who has not defined clear personal goals in comparison with an employee who has determined to build his own home in the next 5 years, will exhibit different level of involvement and zeal at their work. And that's exactly why you need to create the mindset of having targets and fulfilling them even in their personal Lives. Once their thinking process is tuned to be Goal Oriented with accountability, this will have a positive impact on their Targets at Work too.

Setting Future Goals for Every Year: Future Goals can also be termed as Career Management.

Related to their Office, Work, and Career.

Tip: When all these things are achieved – Their job satisfaction will reach all-time high.

- ✓ What do I want to Achieve in my Work?
- ✓ Career Goals
- ✓ Business Volume
- ✓ Sales Volume
- ✓ Productivity
- ✓ Turnover
- ✓ Profitability
- ✓ Adding Clients
- ✓ Expanding Business
- ✓ Certifications

** You can also list down these Goals and set Holistic Goals each Year.

91 FAMILY GOALS

Work-life Balance – Everyone talks about this. Your organization can practice this by motivating People to set holistic goals in their life year on year.

It all starts from you. As business leaders, you lead by example in creating Holistic Goals and achieving them year on year.

Some Creative Inputs for Family Goals
(Remember G = N + D)

- ✓ Spending time with Kids (1 Hr a Day / 5 Hrs a Week)
- ✓ Assisting in their Home Work
- ✓ Household Chores / Helping with Passion
- ✓ Time with Life Partner
- ✓ Time with Parents
- ✓ Weekly Once - Dine Out
- ✓ Monthly Picnic / Outings
- ✓ Annual Tour
- ✓ National /International Tour
- ✓ Visiting Relatives Place
- ✓ Making 30+ Birthday Calls Every Year
- ✓ Daily / Weekly / Monthly - Calling / To be Visited List
- ✓ Sharing in Family WhatsApp or FB Groups
- ✓ Building a Family List / Database to be invited for all Occasions
- ✓ Family Tree

92 FRIENDS GOALS

Family + Friends Goals can be Termed as Relationship Management.

Some Creative Inputs for Friends Goals
(Remember G = N + D)

- ✓ Close Friends Circle
- ✓ Visiting / Calling Schedule
- ✓ Annual Gathering / Trips
- ✓ Birthday Calls
- ✓ Sharing in WhatsApp or FB Groups
- ✓ Visiting Friends Home
- ✓ Inviting Friends to Home
- ✓ Seasonal Gifts

One of the most simple and useful things I have experienced as part of setting a doable goal for family and friends is this . . .

Must Do:

- Note down the Birthdays of your close Family Members and Friends
- Add them on your Personal Calendar
- Just call them on their Birthdays – It is funny how we have even missed these basic things and talk about work-life balance.

** You can also do this for your clients

93 FITNESS GOALS

Those who are physically fit will also be mentally strong. It is essential for every leader to celebrate life hale and healthy.

Some Creative Inputs for Health Goals
(Remember G = N + D)

- ✓ No of Kg to be Reduced
- ✓ No of Kg to be Increased
- ✓ Daily 30 Min of Physical Activity - Walking / Jogging / Cycling / Gym / Yoga
- ✓ Healthy Food (Raw - Semi Cooked - Steamed - Boiled - Pan Fried - Deep Fried)
- ✓ No of times having Oily food in a Week
- ✓ No of times having Non-Veg in a Week
- ✓ Having 3 Meals a Day / Not Skipping Break Fast
- ✓ Donate Blood (Once or Twice in a Year)
- ✓ Water Intake- Adequate Level
- ✓ Health Check Up (Once or Twice in a Year)
- ✓ Swimming (Once or Twice in a Month)
- ✓ Medical Insurance - MUST

** Remember. If a vehicle's parts are worn out, we can get OE Parts (Original Equipment) to replace them.

There are no OE Parts for the human body! It is Natural and God-given. Staying healthy is also showing gratitude to God for what He has given you.

94 FUN GOALS

Beat the Stress – Celebrate Life to the fullest. Set FUN Goals – One of the best gifts you can give to yourself as rewards for accomplishing great things.

Some Creative Inputs for Fun Goals (Employee Level Inputs) (Remember G = N + D)

- ✓ Bucket List (Things to be done Once in a Life Time)
- ✓ Fly in a Plane / Fly with your Family
- ✓ Go for a Foreign Trip
- ✓ Eat in a Star Hotel / Take Family to a Star Hotel
- ✓ Weekly Once - Movie
- ✓ Weekly Once - Play Games (Outdoor and Indoor)
- ✓ Tours, Trips, Eating Out
- ✓ Try Cooking at Home
- ✓ Going to Theme Parks (Once or Twice in a Year)
- ✓ Fly in a Parachute
- ✓ Sky Diving
- ✓ Snorkeling
- ✓ Under Water / Sea Walk
- ✓ Deep Sea Dive with a Life Jacket (With Guards)

** Picture this - Getting back to work after a boring holiday spent hours watching TV vs. Getting back to work after a WOW holiday with Sky Diving and such exciting things.

Fun Matters in Life. Happy Employees are Productive Employees.

95 FINANCE GOALS

Let Money work for you. Your earnings can earn further for you – Save, Invest, Celebrate Life.

Some Creative Inputs for Finance Goals (Employee Level Inputs) (Remember G = N + D)

- ✓ Amount to be Saved for the Year
- ✓ Monthly Investment Target
- ✓ Fixed Deposit
- ✓ Recurring Deposit
- ✓ Bonds
- ✓ Gold Purchase
- ✓ Chit Funds
- ✓ SIP (Must do after finishing basic Savings Plans)
- ✓ Life Insurance - Money Back Policy
- ✓ Life Insurance – (Term Plan / Risk Only Policy)
- ✓ Your Life Risk Value = 1 Year Salary * 20 Times
- ✓ Internet Banking and Mobile Banking in all / main accounts
- ✓ Pay Taxes / EMIs and maintain minimum balance regularly (Good Financial Profile)

** For Sure your family members will be happy to set the Financial Goals along with you.

96 FOCUS AND FAITH GOALS

Faith Goals are your Spiritual Goals. Growing in Spiritual Maturity makes you live a Purposeful Live.

Focus Goals are your Special Goals that don't fall under the other 6 Fs which could be Learning a New Music, a New Language, etc.

Some Inputs for Focus and Faith Goals
(Remember G = N + D)

Faith

- ✓ Daily Meditation
- ✓ Daily Prayers
- ✓ Weekly Visit to Holy Places
- ✓ Holy Trip
- ✓ Offering
- ✓ Volunteering

Focus Areas

- ✓ Extra-Curricular Targets
- ✓ Learn to play a Musical Instrument / Pass in a Grade
- ✓ Learn Driving / Get a License
- ✓ Learn a Language / Join a Course

** Time for Holistic Development of Human Resources in your Organization.

NEW PARADIGM

97 TASK MANAGER AS PERSONAL ACCOUNTABILITY

During the VAT Meeting format, we talked about Task Meetings and Declaring Daily Tasks as a Team. Every individual should get better at Managing their Tasks – This increases Personal Accountability.

"The most matured person is someone who doesn't let others question on their Commitments."

There are two types of people when it comes to Task Management.

- You assign a Task to them; you can rest assured that it will happen no matter what. You can forget about it or consider it done.
- You assign a Task to them; you are going to be worried about that getting done. Need several follow-ups and even set reminders to follow up closely.

What differentiates these two types of People?

For former type has an excellent Task Management System.

Everyone in your Organization needs to practice this not only for the work sake but also for their personal life. Consider that How they treat their personal tasks is how they will treat official tasks as well.

** Let people have a Personal Task Manager and an Official Task Manager.

Tips:

- ✓ Love your Task List because as long as you live, you are going to have a list of things to do!
- ✓ Separate your Task lists as Short Term and Long Term.
- ✓ Plan your Tasks for the day including Short Term Tasks as well as look back for carry forwards from yesterday's Tasks.

Sample Template for Task Management:

My Today	Short Term (1 Week to 3 Months)	Long Term (3 Months+)

** You can also alternatively explore other Tasks and Applications. But never compromise on this.

Most people know what they need to do to become Successful. They just lack a system that makes them take action and progress forward.

98 FAIL ROYALLY

Failing Royally should be part of the culture of your organization. What is Failing Royally? It is to do everything within our limit – Leaving no stone unturned.

Depending on the conviction level, people lose hearts at different point of time.

- ✓ Some people lose the hope of Winning in the last week of the month – They think they can make it up next month.
- ✓ Some people lose the hope of Winning during middle of the month – They think they have to face failure this month.
- ✓ Some people lose the hope of Winning in the very first week of the month – They think this month too is going to be like the last month.

What a Real Leader does?

If 30th evening 10.00 P.M. is the deadline to reach the Goals, they work with full involvement and conviction of making it to success till 9.59 P.M. – Now that's Inspiring!

Opinion – They think it may or may not happen.
Believe – Positively believe it will happen.
Conviction – 100% Belief without Doubts. Believe like Reality!

** You and your People must believe with conviction that your Vision will come true. This is empower you to keep taking action and progress towards the future.

99 GOLDEN LION FORMULA

Here is a short story for you and this is pure imagination. Once a boy was playing at the lawn outside his home. He had some of his favorite toys with him.

After finishing his play time, as he was packing up his toys and putting them inside the toy bag one by one, he found a miniature Lion statue. But it was looking very dirty and seemed like it was made of clay. He had it for a day, and since it was not all that attractive, he threw it over the neighbor's garden.

There was another boy in that home, and he happened to find this toy during his play time. He planned to give a good wash to this toy. He used soap and scrubber to clean it. As he was cleaning, the muddy part chipped away.

He thought he had broken the miniature statue, but to his surprise, it was shining where it got chipped. With curiosity, he tried to remove that entire outer layer and found that it was a Golden Lion!

Well, coming to the point, every employee in your Organization is like that Golden Lion. It is our responsibility to help them discover their best potential, evolve and grow with us!

** Don't judge your Employees. Help them discover their best. Remember someday somebody once trusted you and that's why you are here.

100 THE TWO TOOLS FOR CXO'S

This is one of my favorite concepts. There are two essential tools to be used by every Entrepreneur. It may sound funny, but this is what is needed for success.

The two tools for CXOs are Fuel & Match Stick. Yes, absolutely! When I say Fuel and Match Stick, don't take it literally. Take it in the sense that, you are the Chief Energy Officer for your team. You need to have that Burning Desire to Win and ignite people with that fire (Burning Desire to Win).

Your team can be facing one of the toughest challenges that they have ever encountered but when you walk into the room, you are just setting people on fire. *(Boost the Morale, increase their confidence, get them to believe We Can and It is Possible)*

You are the Energy of your Team.
If your energy is high, their energy is high.
If your energy is low, their energy is low.

I am sure you can point some of your Ex- Bosses who lit that Fire in you every time you had an interaction with them. It's time for you to be that Person as it is Essential for Accelerating Fast Track Growth.

** Keep that Fire Burning!

Thanks for Reading! Time for Implementing ☺

BSB

The most sought after Signature Program of James Vineeth

Business Scale-Up Bootcamp (BSB)

Run Your Business in Auto Pilot Mode!

For CXO's who are looking to Grow Exponentially yet Systematically!

Businesses are meant to Soar New Heights by Providing Solutions for today's Problems and having a Strategy to Evolve along with the ever-changing Local Trends and yet maintain Global Standards. Well, to Empower Entrepreneurs and CXOs to Scale-Up Rapidly, Business Coach James Vineeth has crafted BSB - Business Scale-Up Bootcamp, an Intense High Impact Business Transformation Module with 16 Essential Phases to Build a Business that is Poised to Grow in any Economic Condition

Who can Attend this Program?

- ✓ Entrepreneurs who are looking to Scale up Exponentially yet Systematically!
- ✓ Run a Fool Proof Business that is Conditioned to Succeed in all Economic Conditions
- ✓ Run Business based on Systems through Business Automation Technique
- ✓ CXO Level Leaders - CEO, COO, CTO, VP & Heads

- ✓ Young Entrepreneurs taking Over their Family Business
- ✓ First Generation Entrepreneurs / Well Established Entrepreneurs looking for Next Level
- ✓ Business Leaders who are Hungry for Entrepreneur Gyan / Insights
- ✓ CXOs who are Passionate to Learn New Trends & Practical Insights to Implement in Business.

Save Time, Energy & Money

Save Time

There are 16 Areas that are Essential for Scaling-Up.

It would take at least 5 to 10 years to Gain those Insights one by one from your Own Breakdowns.

#BSB will give you those insights at the intense Bootcamp!

Save Energy

Well, if you are interested, we can even share those 16 Areas, and you can figure them out on your Own. But you need to Spend at-least 2 to 4 Weeks in R&D, E-Learning to understand the concepts and much more time to develop an implementation plan.

#BSB will do it for you!

Save Money

Each Mistake will cost you Money and Growth (Opportunity Loss). Check out for the Next BSB at your City / Scheduled to happen Digitally and avail the Early Bird Offer. That will be the best gift you can give your Business for the FY.

#BSB can SKYROCKET your Business!

Scan the QR Code to Learn More about BSB

GLOSSARY

7F Goals – Future, Family, Friends, Fun, Fitness, Fun & Faith
Action Targets – Actions to be taken to reach the End Results

BOSP – Business Operational Success Plan
BSB – Business Scale-Up Bootcamp
BTG - Breakthrough Goal

CLC – Career Ladder Chart
C.R.M. – Customer Relationship Management
CXO - CEO / COO /CTO / CFO / CLO

ERP – Enterprise Resource Planning
HRM – Human Resource Management
JD – Job Description
KO – Key Outcome
KPI – Key Performance Indicators
LeGroMa – Learning Growth Map
MIS – Management Information System
OP Margin – Operational Margin
OE – Original Equipment

PGP – Personal Growth Plan
P.M. – Possibility Making Machine
POA – Product Offering Analysis
Results Targets - End Results
ROI – Return on Investment
R.P.R.M. - Receive Pressure, Release Motivation

SET - Simplified Expenses Tracker
SBU – Strategic Business Unit
SOP – Standard Operating Procedure
SPME - Simplified Per Month Expense
SSG - Sure Shot Goal
SWOT – Strengths, Weaknesses, Opportunities & Threats
TOPA – Top of the Mind Attention
VAT Meetings – Vision, Action & Task Meetings

ABOUT JAMES VINEETH

James Vineeth is a renowned Business Coach, Author, and Philanthropist. He coaches Entrepreneurs and CXOs on Scaling-Up, Visionary Leadership, Building Social Influence, High Ticket Sales, Personal Excellence, Growth Hacking & Self Mastery through practical tools from Management, Psychology and his own Wisdom Insights Evolved from a Rich R&D of 15+ Years and a wide Exposure of Coaching 125+ Categories and Segments of Companies across different Countries!

People love to attend his workshops because it is simple enough to practice and deep enough to produce results. He connects so well with the audience and delivers high impact and action driven Power Talks.

Through his Sessions and Workshops, James has trained and Coached Lakhs of people on Mastering the aspects of Growing to the Next Level. His Purpose and Mission in life is to not only help everyone to Dream; But to help them follow their Dreams!

Vision 2035

- Empower 1 Lakh CXOs to Scale-Up and Run their Business in Auto Pilot Mode
- Transform 1 Million Leaders through Masterclass and Special Programs
- Impact 10 Million Lives through Digital Medium

Current Responsibilities

- CEO, Revelation Consulting - Coaching & Training
- CEO, SJ Brand Studio –Branding Solutions
- Managing Trustee, STG – Youth Development NGO
- Head PR – HUWAD – Child Rights NGO
- Board Member - Select Institutions & Organizations

James' Signature Events

- How to SELL like Hot Cakes?
  Sales Excellence Masterclass
- Building Better Leaders
  Leadership Excellence Masterclass
- Business Scale-Up Bootcamp
  Intense Coaching for Entrepreneurs & CXOs

Offerings

- PEP UP My Team – High Energy Sessions for Corporates
- Keynote Address for Awards Day, Product Launch, Dealers Meets, and Corporate Gatherings
- BEC - Business Empowerment Coaching (Blend of CEO Coaching & Staff Training with Growth Consulting)
- KPI Consulting – Gamify Your Business
- LeGroMa – Custom Crafted Gamified Learning Growth Map for Large Corporations.

www.jamesvineeth.com

www.ingramcontent.com/pod-product-compliance
Lightning Source LLC
Chambersburg PA
CBHW022147160726
48282CB00024B/206
* 9 7 8 9 3 5 3 4 6 1 7 4 4 *